THEN AND THERE SERIES
GENERAL EDITOR
MARJORIE REEVES, M.A. Ph.D.

Josiah Wedgwood and the Potteries

S. M. ARCHER, M. A.

Senior History Master
Batley Grammar School

Illustrated from contemporary sources

LONGMAN

LONGMAN GROUP LIMITED
London
Associated companies branches and representatives
throughout the world

© *Longman Group Ltd 1973*

First published 1973

ISBN 0 582 20431 3

Photoset in Malta by St Paul's Press Ltd
Printed in Hong Kong by Sheck Wah Tong Printing Press

For E. McNeil

Contents

Josiah Wedgwood (1730–95), from the portrait by Sir Joshua Reynolds

To the Reader

Thousands of years ago prehistoric man probably discovered by accident how to make pots. He may have noticed that a footprint in the clay became hard baked in the sun, and held water for a long time. He would soon begin to make his own clay containers. People have been making pots ever since and *archaeologists**** now use the pieces of pottery which they find in their 'digs' to help date their discoveries.

Perhaps you have tried to make some pottery in your school art or craft room. Even if you were not very successful, you will probably admit that you do not need very expensive or complicated machinery – only some clay, an oven, and a wheel on which to turn the clay so that it can be shaped and moulded by the hands as the flat disc revolves. If making pottery is so ancient and so easy you may be wondering why Josiah Wedgwood, who died less than two hundred years ago, is an important figure in the history of pottery.

One reason is that the everyday use of pottery in English kitchens and dining rooms is not very old. In 1750 rich nobles and merchants ate or drank from silver, *pewter* or glass. The poor used leather 'bottles' and wooden jugs, basins and plates. It was largely due to Wedgwood's work that the use of cups and saucers, plates and bowls, became both popular and practical. Josiah Wedgwood made many other objects in pottery. He was very proud of his beautiful vases. When he died in 1795 he had become 'Vasemaker general to the Universe'.

The object of this book is to show how he did it, and how he 'astonished the world all at once'.

*Words printed in *italics* in the text are explained in the Glossary, p. 110.

Blunging the clay in a pot-works in the 1850s.
The process remained basically the same as in domestic industry

This print from the 1850s shows a woman turning the wheel for the thrower
and a boy in the centre wedging the clay into balls

1 *The Staffordshire Pottery Industry before Wedgwood*

Potters had been working in North Staffordshire for many years before Josiah Wedgwood was born in 1730. There was plenty of wood and coal to heat the ovens, there were many different types of clay conveniently near the surface, and there was running water to use in washing and preparing the clay. A typical pottery in 1700 was a small thatched cottage with lean-to working sheds covered by turf. Nearby there would be a small oven, about eight feet high and six feet wide, and this too would be surrounded by *sods* to keep the heat in.

Clay was dug from the local pits, but it had to be carefully prepared before it could be used. The potter 'blunged' it in a tank about twenty feet square and eighteen inches deep, beating it about in water with a huge wooden oar, so that any stones fell to the bottom. When dry it was cut and stored in a damp cellar. Any air bubbles were driven out by 'wedging'. The clay was cut with wires, and one piece was lifted above the head and thrown down on top of the other several times. It was then kneaded like dough and made into balls. The potter would then *throw* his piece on the wheel, while the clay was shaped into a jug or cup, or whatever was needed. After drying, the pieces were taken to a 'stouking' shed, where a worker called a stouker made the handles and fixed them to the pieces, which were finally given a coat of liquid clay, or dusted with powdered lead if a shiny surface was wanted.

The pieces were now ready for the oven. The fire was lit on Friday and the pots were placed in fire-proof containers called 'saggars' and carefully arranged in the oven. The last stoking would take place early on Sunday, and the oven was left to cool

A crateman on the road. Pottery was distributed by such families

for at least ten hours before the pieces were taken out on Monday morning. If the potter had prepared his clay well and kept the oven at the right heat, he would now have a good quantity of finished pottery. Mistakes were often made, however, and heaps of broken pot were a familiar sight.

'Cratemen' then loaded the pottery on to mules, or carried it on their backs to the local villages, farms and towns. The potters in 1700 only supplied the needs of their surrounding countryside, and many pot works were family affairs. Sons dug the clay, father made the pots, and the women packed the crates. English pottery had not yet reached the tables of great houses. Brown butter pots and other useful articles for farms and cottages were too rough and ready for the rich.

Yet these small-scale producers were already experimenting and trying out new ideas. In 1693 two Dutch brothers, John and Philip Elers, had set up a pot works in North Staffordshire. By carefully preparing their clay and by skilful decoration, they made high quality pottery – especially their fine red tea-pots which became famous even outside Staffordshire. They tried to keep their improvements secret, and only employed 'dull witted' workmen who could not explain the new ideas to others. However, these attempts at secrecy failed, for two local potters are said to have pretended to be idiots, worked for the brothers and discovered their improvements. More and more potters began to experiment.

In the next sixty years there were many changes. John Astbury found in 1720 that if flint-stones were ground into powder and mixed with the clay a whiter, stronger pottery could be made. Twelve years later Thomas Benson invented a method of grinding the flint under water to avoid damage to the potters' lungs from the dust. Ralph Shaw of Burslem invented a method of drying the clay in kilns rather than leaving it out in the sun and exposing it to impurities. Ovens were improved so that the temperature was easier to control. Enoch Booth of Tunstall began to use the pure white clays of Devon and Cornwall and started the process of firing the pottery twice – once to harden the clay, giving it a '*biscuit*' texture, and secondly to give it a final glassy or decorated finish (it was then called *glazed*).

This teapot, made in 1761, shows the love of Chinese decorations. It was made from porcelain and, as the cracks suggest, was too fragile for everyday use

9

These Staffordshire potters were trying to imitate the beautifully delicate 'china' or porcelain which was coming into England from the east. (Porcelain is very thin, fine pottery fired at great heat: the Chinese were expert at making it.) Any new idea which helped men like Astbury, Benson, Shaw and Booth was quickly copied. Change was becoming an accepted and normal fact.

It was Josiah Wedgwood who quickened the changes, improved the quality and increased the output of Staffordshire pottery. By 1790 men all over the world spoke of Wedgwood*ware* rather than pottery. Wedgwoodware was used in English and Russian palaces, in European inns, hotels and country houses, and in the newly independent world of North America. A local craft in 1730 had become an international industry by 1790.

2 The Young Josiah

Wedgwood was born in 1730 at Burslem, one of the six towns now forming the county borough of Stoke-on-Trent, and known today as 'the Potteries'.

Josiah claimed in later life that he was 'born on the lowest rung of the ladder', but he was perhaps exaggerating a little in order to make his eventual rise to fame and wealth appear even more impressive. In fact his father was a fairly prosperous potter who owned his own house and works. However, as Josiah was the youngest of thirteen children, and as his father died when the boy was only nine years old, the claim that he was a self-made man can be reasonably accepted.

At the age of six, Josiah began his schooling. He had to walk seven miles to a school at Newcastle-under-Lyme, but he left after three years on his father's death. For the next five years he helped his brothers in the family pot-works and he must have been a promising boy, for when he was fourteen he was *apprenticed* to his eldest brother, Thomas. Here are some of the promises which Josiah, his mother, and Thomas had to make:

> Josiah Wedgwood with the consent and direction of his mother, hath put and doth hereby binde himself Apprentice unto Thomas Wedgwood, to learn his Art, Mystery, Occupation or Employment of Throwing and Handling . . .
>
> With him as an Apprentice to dwell, continue and serve from the date hereof (11th November 1744), unto the full end and term of five years from thence ensuing . . .
>
> At Cards, Dice, or any other unlawful Games, he shall not play:

Taverns or ale house he shall not frequent:
Matrimony he shall not contract.

If he kept these promises, Josiah would be given in return a training in how to throw pots and, 'Meat, Drink, Washing and lodging, and *Apparel* of all kinds, both Linen and Woollen, and all other necessaries'. However, he would be paid no wages. This kind of apprenticeship was slowly dying out – especially as some boys found it so annoying to have to work for nothing that they did as much damage as possible to their master's products, so that he would be only too glad to end the contract before the full five years was up.

Josiah, however, was no such rebel. He worked very hard and became quite skilful, but at the age of seventeen he was attacked by smallpox. This dreaded disease was much more common in the eighteenth century than it is now, and it often left its victims disfigured or disabled. This is not surprising when methods of treatment are examined. One short sharp cure was 'Mice, fried alive'. A longer and even more horrible remedy was to 'Take thirty or forty live toads, burn them in a new pot to black cinders or ashes, and make them into a fine powder. Add live earthworms, hog-lice, frog's liver. Dose to be taken three times a day.'

Josiah survived, despite such barbarous treatment, but his left leg was weak and painful, and he had to work with it resting on a stool. He was still very interested in his work, especially in trying out new ideas to improve pottery. He studied colouring and decoration and spent a great deal of time experimenting to try to produce a whiter finish. His brother, however, was not very pleased with the new methods, and after the five years were up he refused to allow Josiah to become his partner. For the next two years Josiah worked for wages, and by 1752 he had saved enough money to enter into an unsuccessful partnership with John Harrison. After two years he left Harrison and became the partner of Thomas Whieldon, a rich, experienced and well-known potter. This partnership lasted five years, until in 1759 Josiah had saved enough money to be able to start up in Burslem in business on his own. He rented the Ivy House

The Brick House or Bell Works, Burslem

works, which consisted of two ovens, a shed, a workhouse and a small cottage, and began to make brilliantly clear green pottery, in leaf and vegetable shapes, cauliflower and cabbage, fir cone, lettuce and tomato patterns. Three years later he moved to the bigger 'Bell works', to which his workers were called by a bell instead of the usual horn.

Josiah had by now shown that, despite his illness and handicap, he was hard-working, skilful and enthusiastic about new ideas and experiments in the pottery industry. Luckily, things were happening in the world outside Burslem which could help an ambitious young potter.

3 The New Markets

Even before 1700 Britain was slowly changing from an agricultural rural country into one which was active in trade and industry. One historian, Charles Wilson, has written of the period 1600 to 1760 as the apprenticeship of the nation before it reached eventual industrial mastery. Certainly, after 1760, the changes were much faster. An American writer, Walter Rostow, compares these changes to the flight of an aeroplane – before flying the plane needs to build up speed on a long runway, just as this country was preparing for many years before the final take-off into industrialisation.

These changes, which made Britain into a country of cotton factories and coal mines, cities and iron works, are called 'the Industrial Revolution', and the fact that they were beginning when Josiah Wedgwood set up on his own is an important reason for his astonishing success.

By 1760 English people were becoming richer. Many still lived and worked in very bad conditions, in old villages as well as growing towns. Yet our trade with other countries was growing rapidly – and the money we made by selling abroad, or by carrying the goods of other countries in our ships, helped almost everyone. A farmer's wife and children could add to the family income by preparing wool for spinning and weaving. The farmer could use better farming methods and grow extra food which he sold to the people in towns and cities. More and more people were earning wages which left them with more money than they needed purely for essentials like food, clothes and shelter. This extra money could be used to buy things which were previously impossible for them to possess – luxuries such as new pottery or ornaments.

Spinning yarn in the cottage. The woman in the centre is boiling the yarn, the woman on the right is putting it on to reels. This print gives perhaps a cheerful view of domestic conditions

15

Not only was there more money to buy pottery – there were more people to use it. The population, which had been growing very slowly for over a thousand years, suddenly began to grow more quickly. In 1750 there were about 6½ million people in England and Wales. This means that, in proportion, out of a modern class of thirty school-children, there would only have been three or four children alive then. By 1801, when the first accurate census or count was taken, there were nearly 9 million people. By 1850 the population explosion had reached 18 million. Such an increase not only meant that more people wanted to buy goods – there were also more workers to make them.

People who lived at the time realised that this increase was occurring, but they did not know why. Some of them, like Thomas Malthus, gloomily believed that it would end in starvation. Others like Horace Walpole, youngest son of the famous

London in 1746 from the terrace of Richmond House. A painting by Canaletto. Notice St Paul's Cathedral in the distance

politican Robert, could only wonder at the effect of the rise on cities such as London. In 1776 he boasted that 'London could put Florence into its *fob pocket*'. Fifteen years later he was still amazed:

> There will soon be one street from London to Brentford, ay, and from London to every village miles around. . . . Nor is there any complaint of *depopulation* from the country. Bath shoots out into new crescents, circuses and squares every year. Birmingham, Manchester, Hull and Liverpool would serve any king in Europe for a capital and would make the Empress of Russia's mouth water.

The increasing demand for pottery brought by this population rise was strengthened by changes in the habits and tastes of people – especially by changes in their drinking habits.

People who had been accustomed to drinking beer, wine or spirits began to drink more and more tea and coffee. Beer had been the normal drink of Englishmen for centuries. When houses were cold and dirty, work dreary and boring, people turned to alcohol as a means of escape. Workers would often work till their pockets were full and then drown their sorrows. Heavy drinking was often found amongst the rich as well as the poor. 'Drunk as a lord' was a phrase first used in the eighteenth century. Horace Walpole described how, after a ball, 'Lincoln, Lord Holderness, Lord Robert Sutton, young Churchill and a dozen more grew jolly, stayed till seven in the morning and drank thirty-two bottles'.

By 1750 such heavy drinking was becoming rarer. The price of spirits rose as a result of government taxes. The ships of the East India Company were sailing to China and returning with chests of tea. Coffee, chocolate and tea slowly became cheaper and more popular, so that all but the very poor drank them. In London, coffee houses became centres of social life. Each had its own particular type of customer, from artists to politicians, from merchants to lawyers. One of them, run by Edward Lloyd, was the place where the latest news of the progress of ships at sea could be obtained. Lloyd's Insurance company started 17

An early London coffee house. Notice the man pouring coffee in the centre and the news sheets on the table

Taking tea. This family was rich enough to afford porcelain cups and saucers

there, as ship-owners were anxious to spread their losses or guard their profits by selling shares in the value of their ships.

Our modern fame as a tea-drinking nation began in this century. Dr Johnson, the great writer and conversationalist, 'drank great quantities of it at all hours'. As early as 1730 a Dr Deering had grumbled that in Nottingham, 'even a common washerwoman thinks she has not had a proper breakfast without Tea, and hot, buttered white bread'. New kinds of cups were needed to serve such polite drinks. The old pottery was too crude and rough. It would scratch the polished tables and wear away the silver spoons of the rich. Chinese porcelain was too fine and delicate to stand up to hard wear. Silver was too dear for most people.

A fortune could be made by the man who first made cups and saucers, bowls and plates, which were strong, attractive and easy to handle. Josiah Wedgwood succeeded in doing this – and he died worth £500,000.

4 New Pottery, New Partners

After 1759, when he set up in business on his own, Josiah had been constantly trying to improve the quality of his 'useful' pottery. He had made over seven thousand experiments with different types of clay at varying temperatures. In 1763 at last he produced a hard wearing, reasonably attractive pottery by mixing ground flint, local clay and kaolin, an extremely white clay from Cornwall. Although it does not appear very exciting by today's standards, it was much smoother and shinier than anybody else's useful pottery at that time. Wedgwood proudly described it as 'a type of earthenware for the table, quite new in appearance, covered with a rich and brilliant glaze, bearing sudden alterations of heat and cold, made quickly and easily, and consequently cheap.'

The new Queen's Ware

He presented a breakfast set of the new pottery or 'creamware' to Queen Charlotte and she was so pleased with it that she ordered a complete table service. Josiah obtained her permission to call his discovery 'Queen's Ware', and in 1765 he began to print, 'Josiah Wedgwood, Potter to Her Majesty', on his bills. At thirty-five, he had at last arrived! Although

Etruria in Staffordshire Augst 2nd 1783
Mr Smee
Bought of Josiah Wedgwood,
Potter to her Majesty
N.B. His Manufacture is sold at his Warehouse at Portland House in Greek Street Soho London, & at Mr. Neunburgs No. 75 Cornhill, & at no other Place in Town; & as he now sells for Ready Money only, he delivers the Goods safe and carriage free to London.

brown & green Gardenpots — 0 14 0
2 fawn & white fluted — 0 7 0
£1 1 0

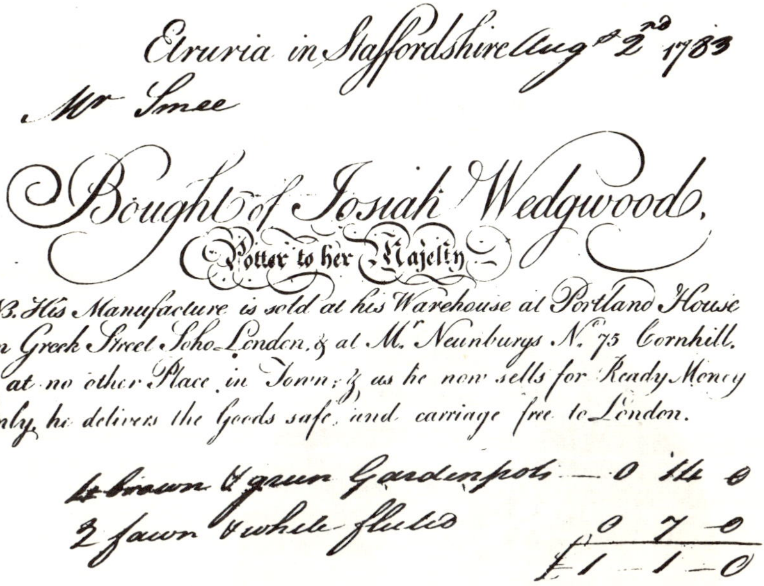

A bill from the Potter to her Majesty

Wedgwood later made many other changes in pottery, this first improvement – Queen's Ware – was his greatest single success. He had put fine useful pottery within reach of the pockets of almost everyone – and almost everyone began to buy it. As he wrote to Thomas Bentley in 1769: 'The demand for this cream colour, or Queen's Ware, still increases. It is really amazing how rapidly the use of it has spread almost over the whole globe, and how *universally* it is liked.'

A NEW PARTNER

Thomas Bentley was an old friend of Josiah's. They had first met in Liverpool, where Bentley was a merchant, on one of

Josiah's visits to the firm which decorated some of his pottery by transferring prints on to it. Wedgwood had been thrown from his horse, and whilst he recovered and rested his weak leg, he had made friends with Bentley.

The injury to his leg was never completely cured. In 1768 it was causing Josiah so much pain when he walked that he decided to have the leg cut off and replaced by a wooden one. This was a brave decision to take, especially as there were no pain-killers in those days and there was the possibility of death if the wound did not heal properly. However, Josiah survived and later referred cheerfully to the 28th of May 1768, as 'St Amputation Day'.

Josiah became more and more impressed with Bentley, for this Liverpool merchant had all the skills which the potter would have loved to possess. Bentley was well educated, and

Thomas Bentley, who helped Wedgwood sell to the rich and noble. This is a photograph of one of Wedgwood's cameos in jasper. Notice the love of Roman dress

knew about books and plays, opera and music, art and sculpture. He spoke good French and Italian. He also had experience of the practical side of business – keeping accounts of sales and profits. As Josiah was becoming busier and busier, experimenting, organising his works and collecting money, he began to understand how valuable Bentley could be to him. In 1768 he persuaded Bentley to join him as a partner in the sale of his ornamental pottery – for as we shall see later, Bentley could help and advise on how best to obtain the custom of the rich and fashionable.

MARRIAGE AND CHILDREN

Wedgwood did find time for other things apart from work. On 25 January 1765 he had married his third cousin, Sarah Wedgwood. The marriage was very happy and they had eight child-

Sarah Wedgwood

ren, some of whom became quite famous themselves. The eldest, Susannah, became the mother of a very famous scientist, Charles Darwin. John, the eldest son, began the Royal Horticultural (gardening) Society. Josiah, the second son, took over the pottery business. Thomas, the third son, became a scientist himself and was one of the early inventors of photography.

Perhaps the success of the children was partly due to their father's interest in their schooling. Like many other people at this time Josiah could not find a suitable school for his children. The famous 'public' or boarding schools were not in very good condition – soldiers had had to be called in to some to crush schoolboy riots. Most of the old grammar schools were also very inefficient, teaching only a smattering of Greek and Latin in decaying, unhealthy buildings. There were many private schools, run to make a profit for the schoolmaster, but the quality of these varied greatly. Josiah decided to try to provide a good education for his children at home. As early as 1769 he employed a French teacher, making certain that the foreigner did not visit his works and take his secrets back to France. Ten years later he had really organised their learning, as we can see in his letter to Bentley on 19 December 1779. Their French and Drawing Master was to be a French prisoner from Lichfield who had received permission to return home if he wanted, but preferred to remain in England in an 'agreeable situation'. Unfortunately this Monsieur Potet did not prove entirely satisfactory, for Josiah complained that, 'he plays his authority away in a boyish manner, and then is obliged to establish it again by thrashing the boys. I will not admit of his striking the boys again on any pretence.'

The Latin master was Thomas Byerley, Josiah's nephew, and a worker in the pottery firm, who later became his partner. The teacher of English and Mathematics ('Writing and Accounts') was Peter Swift, the chief clerk and *accountant* of the firm, whom Josiah described as 'Cashier, Paymaster-General, and Accountant-General . . . without him we should all be in confusion at once'.

Josiah Wedgwood and his family, painted by George Stubbs in 1780 in the gardens of Etruria. From left to right: Mary Anne, Sarah, Thomas, Catherine, Susannah, Josiah II, John, Sarah and Josiah.

Here is Josiah's account of a typical day at his school. Compare it with your own experience, and decide which you prefer.

Rise at 7 in winter, when I shall ring the school bell, and at 6 in summer.

Dress and wash – half an hour.
The boys are then to write with Mr Swift for one hour in some room fitted up for the purpose in the works.
The little girls are to have an English lesson with their nurse in the school, which happens to be a room near the nursery.
Breakfast – as schoolboys, 8.30 to 9.
From 9 to 10, French.
From 10 to 11, Drawing.
From 11 to 1, Riding or other exercise, which will include gardening, *fossilling*, experimenting etc. etc.
From 1 to dinner at half past 1, washing etc. in order to be decent at table.
Half past two, Latin for one hour.
Then French, one hour, and conversation in the same in the fields, garden or elsewhere, half an hour to 5 o'clock.
From 5 to 7, exercise – games of catch or 'tig', etc.
At 7, Accounts for one hour – supper and to bed at 9.

Josiah was obviously determined to make his children work hard at their studies, and he planned to occupy almost every moment of the day. Later he took care to see that they were taught science by experts – he even persuaded a famous Scots chemist, John Leslie, to leave Edinburgh and come down to teach them. The potter who had had little serious education himself was eager to make sure that his children did not suffer in the same way. Perhaps you think that he made them suffer more?

5 The New Works – Etruria

By 1766 Josiah began to plan the building of a new factory, big enough to supply the world with his creamware pottery. In 1769 he bought, for £3,000, the Ridge House Estate, a large area of land between Hanley and Newcastle under Lyme – land which was reasonably flat and good for building.

A Mr Pickford from Derby was employed as the *architect* to plan and build a new Hall for Josiah, a smaller house for Bentley, and a huge new factory. Wedgwood's worries had begun, for he often had to complain about Pickford's work, accusing him of overcharging and bad building. He grumbled that the 'plaistering' peeled off in the Hall, and stated that Bentley's House was not fit to live in for, 'the Wet comes through the roof and down the walls from the Attick to the ground floor'.

Eventually these building problems were sorted out, but Josiah then had to worry about money. He decided to build the factory in two stages – the first stage was to be the Ornamental Works. In June 1769 Josiah opened these first buildings, riding from Burslem with a party of family and friends. The partners made the first vases themselves to celebrate the opening – Thomas turning the wheel and Josiah 'throwing'. Six black vases were thrown and the inscription on them was 'Artes Etruscae Renascuntur' ('the Arts [or skills] of Etruria will be reborn'). Wedgwood chose the name Etruria as a reminder of the Greeks who had made beautiful pottery thousands of years ago – pottery which Josiah was determined to imitate and equal.

Etruria was the name given to an ancient district of central Italy, where many painted Greek vases were found in tombs. 27

The Etruscans, (from whom we have the modern word 'Tuscany'), made beautiful copies of Greek vases and statues.

Four months later the second stage was begun; the building of the 'useful works'. All this must have been a great strain on Josiah's finances for he wrote anxiously to Bentley on 19 November 1769:

> I have been planning the remainder of my works here, which must all be built, besides a Town for the men to live in, by the next summer . . . where shall I get money, materials or hands to finish so much building, in so short a time? . . . Collect, collect my friend – set all your hands and heads to work – send me the money and you shall see wonders. £3,000! £3,000? – aye £3,000 and not a farthing less will satisfy my Architect for the next year's business, so you must either collect or find a place for me with the *bankrupts*.

Josiah's fears and worries proved to be too gloomy and by 1770 his new works were built, if not paid for, and he was the controller of the largest pottery works in Europe. If you visit

Etruria today you will find it very difficult to find anything of this factory still standing. Almost all the buildings have been knocked down and a busy road runs straight through the old estate and village. The level of the old works is now much lower than that of the canal, due to *subsidence* caused by coal mining.

Etruria Hall in 1770

Etruria Hall still stands; it is now used as the offices of an iron company. It is on a slight slope overlooking the works, to the north side of the road to Newcastle. Josiah laid out the area between the Hall and the works as an ornamental garden, with two small lakes near the canal. The Hall is of three *storeys*, with thirty-four rooms, built in the classical style of the Greeks and Romans. In the cellars Josiah had his own private laboratory fitted out, and there is said to have been a secret passage from the Hall to the works. The building must have impressed all who saw it with the riches and ambition of the owner.

An early view of the works at Etruria.
(Notice the bell, the bottle chimneys and
the horse-drawn barge)

There were two main squares to the works, each surrounded by brick buildings or sheds. Black Bank Yard was the centre for ornamental pottery, whilst the useful ware was made in the Big Yard. Wedgwood had by now learnt that the best way to train skilled workers was to divide up the process of pottery making into separate stages and allow each worker to specialise in only one stage. By practice and repetition the worker learned to do his own task quickly and expertly. The works were therefore divided up into separate buildings or sheds, in each of which a separate stage in the manufacture was to be performed. Every shed was a completely separate unit, with its own entrance and outside stairway, so that to move from one shed to another a worker had to go out of doors. The courtyards were *cobbled* and the buildings had small green glass windows. The whole works were surrounded by high walls, except where they were bounded by the canal.

A very early photograph of Etruria. Notice the Hall in the top left corner, the factory with its biscuit and glost ovens in the centre and the first cottages for the workers lining the road to the right

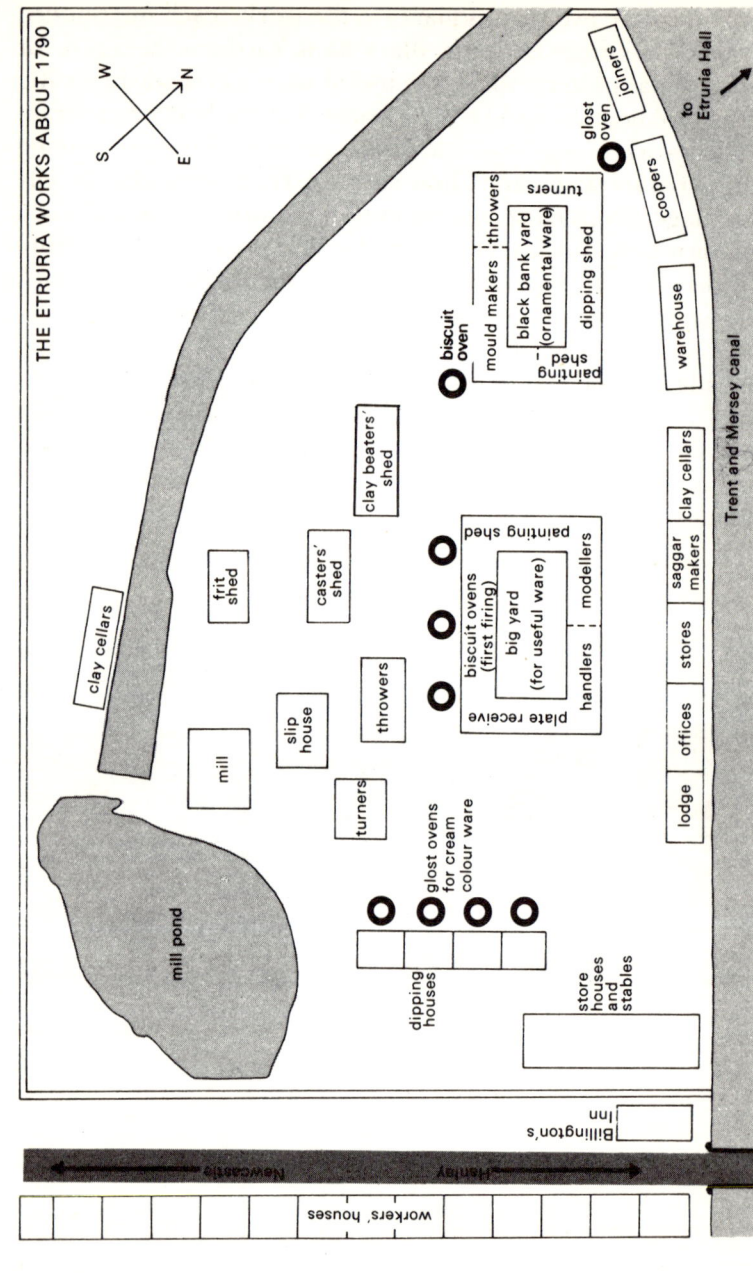

THE ETRURIA WORKS ABOUT 1790

mill pond

clay cellars

mill

frit shed

slip house

casters' shed

clay beaters' shed

turners

throwers

glost ovens for cream colour ware

dipping houses

store houses and stables

biscuit oven

biscuit ovens (first firing)

big yard (for useful ware)

plate receive

handlers   modellers

painting shed

mould makers   throwers

black bank yard (ornamental ware)

turners

dipping shed

painting shed

glost oven

joiners

coopers

warehouse

clay cellars

saggar makers

stores

offices

lodge

Billington's Inn

workers' houses

Newcastle   Henley

Trent and Mersey canal

to Etruria Hall

6 Making Pottery at Etruria

Different types of pottery were made with different types and mixtures or 'bodies' of clay. The local Staffordshire clay had to be mixed with rarer clays to obtain the best results. Wedgwood bought 'kaolin' or china clay from Devon and Cornwall, and even considered buying land in North America which would provide special clays. Sometimes powdered flint or crushed animal bone was mixed with the clays to produce whiter and stronger pottery. Some pottery is therefore called 'bone china'. Earthenware pottery is duller in appearance; stoneware is harder since it is left in the oven longer; porcelain is very fine and delicate pottery made from a very white clay body and fired at extremely high temperatures. The different types of clay body were stored in cellars by the canal, and nearby there was a water mill in which the flints and bones were crushed to powder. Wedgwood, as always eager to improve methods of production, was the first pottery manufacturer to order a steam engine in 1782, from the famous firm of Boulton and Watt, in order to grind the bones and flints more easily. (Indeed Josiah had been so enthusiastic about the possibilities of steam power that he had lent Matthew Boulton £5,000 during the difficult experimental stages of the development of the engine.)

Wedgwood also helped to perfect the 'casting' of pottery. Pots of very complicated shape cannot easily be thrown or shaped by hand, but instead they are cast in moulds – a process similar to the way in which jelly is made. 'Slip' was used for this, a thick creamy mixture of clay, flint, bone and water, made in the 'Slip-House' next to the mill. Nearby there were sheds for modellers, mould-makers, and casters. The modellers

Josiah Wedgwood inspecting ornamental pottery at Etruria. Notice his walking stick by the fire. Perhaps he had already broken the piece lying on the floor!

designed new styles and pieces of pottery, shaping in raw clay to a larger size than the finished piece would be, for they had to allow for the shrinking which took place during firing and drying. A clay mould or impression was taken from the model, and from this a *plaster of Paris* copy was made. This was a skilled job, for the different parts of a mould have to fit together exactly, for a bad join leaves a line or raised seam on the pottery. 'Slip' was then poured into the plaster of Paris mould, and the plaster absorbed the water, so that a thin layer of clay was left lining the inside of the mould. The 'caster' had to be skilled enough to know exactly how long to leave the slip in the mould in order to obtain the required thickness. The clay shrank as it dried, so that the mould could be removed and used again.

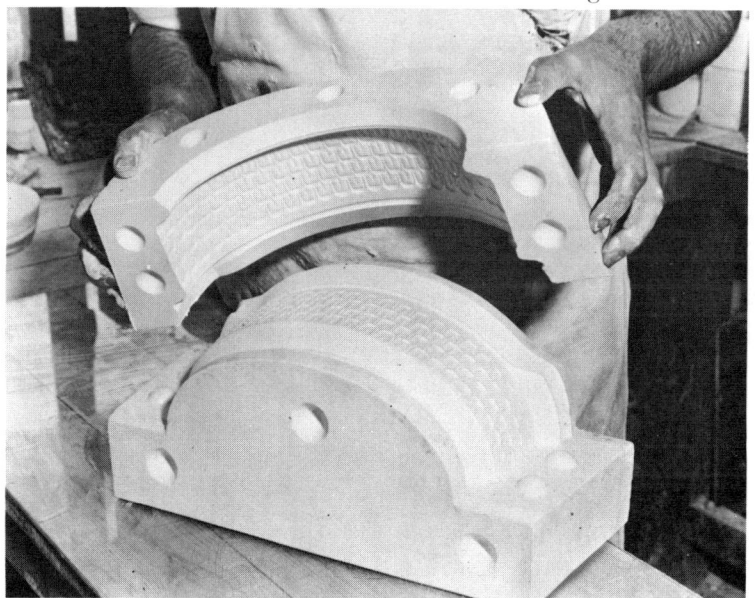

Mould making. Notice how the mould is carefully fitted together by notches and recesses to prevent a bad join

Next to the slip house and casting sheds was the shed for the claybeaters, the descendants of the 'blungers and wedgers' of domestic days. Their job was still to clean the clay and to remove air bubbles. Clay was then taken to the throwing shed

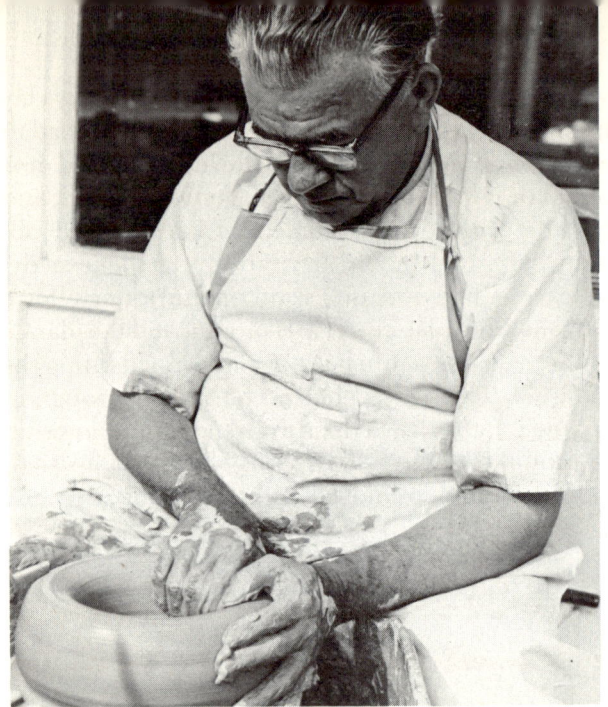

A modern thrower at work

Workmen in the yard of the factory at Etruria

where boys pressed it into balls and turned the wheels for the throwers who shaped the jugs or vases. The clay ball was thrown on to the revolving wheel and shaped into a cone. This cone was opened with the thumb, and with one hand inside and the other outside, the thrower pressed and pulled the clay into shape.

After these wet pieces had dried to a texture like that of cheese, the turners shaped them to the exact thickness and shape wanted. The turner placed the pieces on a lathe which quickly rotated the piece horizontally. Cutting tools were used to trim and pare away the clay, and circular or bead decorations could be made at this stage. Again Josiah was quick to adopt steam-powered lathes for engine-turning.

A turner at work in the late nineteenth century. Note the piece of Jasperware in the background, and the vases ready for the oven in the right corner

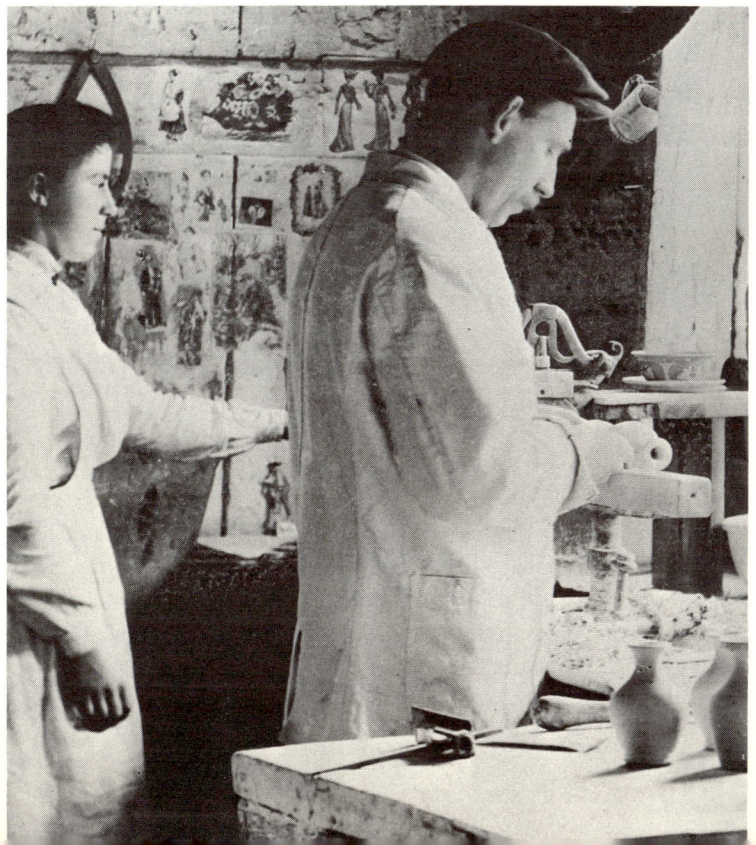

Pieces which needed handles or spouts were then taken to the handling or stouking sheds. Here skilled men fixed them on by using the exact amount of finger pressure and a touch of clay and water. To obtain a good strong join the handle or spout had to be made of exactly the same body of clay as the pieces to which they were fixed. Josiah was very anxious to make certain that his useful ware really was useful – so that the handles had to be put in convenient places, the spouts had to pour without spilling, and lids had to fit securely.

Fixing the handles

The pieces were then placed on trolleys and pushed to the 'receive' shed near the brick-built bottle-shaped ovens. Here they were left to dry until they were white and chalky. They were then ready for the first or biscuit firing, and they were placed in 'saggars' (fire proof clay containers) in a fixed position in the oven. This first firing took about two days, and the pottery had a biscuit texture and appearance when it was re-

moved.

The original biscuit and glost ovens at Etruria, photographed before demolition in the twentieth century

Painters at work in the late nineteenth century. Notice the pattern book from which they worked on the stool, and the finished pieces in the bottom right corner

If the finished pottery was to have a shiny or glossy 'finish' it was then taken to the dipping shed. Here it was dipped in 'frit', a liquid mixture of clay, lead powder and flint. The water dried off, leaving a thin glaze on the pottery, which was carefully brushed and cleaned to leave a surface which would be smooth and sparkling, easy to clean but difficult to damage.

After the frit had dried, pottery which needed decorating was taken to the painting sheds, where special enamel heat-resistant paint was carefully applied by hand. Finally the pottery was taken to the 'glost ovens' for the second firing. This took about thirty hours, at a temperature of about 1,200°C, which was slightly lower than that during the first or biscuit firing.

An oven-man in the nineteenth century. He is resting on saggars, the containers in which the pottery was fired

The completed pottery was then taken to the warehouses by the canal for checking and inspection. The pieces were roughly handled to test their strength, and packed into barrels which were loaded onto barges. These barges would go to many inland towns, and to the great ports of Liverpool, Hull or London — and from there Wedgwood's pottery was sent all over the world.

This survey of the works should give you some idea of the size and complexity of Etruria — but there were other buildings. There were offices for the clerks, and a lodge for the porter. There were sheds for the cooper, who made the barrels, for the saggar-makers, and for the works' joiners. There were store-houses and stables. Even then Wedgwood's building was not finished, for since Etruria was a new and modern factory in the countryside, he had to build houses for his workers to live in. In the next chapter you can find out more about these workers and their houses.

7 Wedgwood's Workers

In 1790 Josiah employed about 220 workers, including boys and girls, at Etruria. By 1816 the number had risen to 387, of whom 13 were under ten, and 103 between ten and eighteen years old. They worked long hours – from 6.30 in the morning to 6 in the evening, and even longer when there were plenty of orders to complete. They had only half an hour's rest for breakfast and one hour for dinner. Most of the workers, however, thought that Josiah was a kind and good employer.

FOOD RIOTS

Perhaps this was because poor people were used to working long hours for low wages. Certainly most people who lived in England before 1760 were very poor. The great differences between the rich and poor were accepted as natural and normal. Indeed some people argued that the poor must be kept poor in order to make them work harder. But wages could be too low, and even Wedgwood at Etruria had occasional trouble. The greatest fear of the rich was the possibility of theft, murder and riot by 'that many headed monster, the mob'. When riots broke out in Etruria in 1783 Josiah stayed firmly on the side of law and order – after all he had much to lose.

A bad harvest had sent food prices rocketing. When a canal boat containing flour and cheese to be taken to Manchester tied up for a short time opposite the canal bridge to Wedgwood's factory, the temptation was too much for the hungry workers. The rioters, led by two men named Barlow and Boulton, took the food and sold it at what they thought was a reasonable price, giving the money to the captain of the barge. A second food barge was treated in the same way. There is some evidence that the leaders also tried to set fire to Wedgwood's works.

The authorities were determined to crush such dangerous behaviour. The army was brought in, and the mob ordered to scatter within one hour. At the end of the hour the soldiers charged, causing much confusion but no deaths. Josiah was in London at the time, but he was told of the riots in letters from his sons, Thomas and John. Here is Tom's letter of 11 March 1783:

Dear Papa,

As I thought you might like to know how the mob went on I will tell you. On Sunday all was quiet. On Monday the mob came to Billington's (the inn next to the works) where there was a meeting of the Master Potters. The mob was told that if they did not *disperse* in an hour's time the soldiers would fire on them . . .

An hour gone by and they did not disperse. The women were much worse than the men, as for example the Parson had got about 30 men to leave and follow him, but a woman cried, 'Nay, nay, that will not do, that will not do', and it was agreed that the corn taken from the boat should be sold at a fair price.

Boulton and Barlow are taken up and gone to Stafford. The rest of the days have been quiet.

P.S. I would have written this letter well, but I have the headache.

This arrest of the ringleaders must have been effective, for John wrote to his father six days later:

I was at Stafford to hear the trial of Boulton and Barlow, the latter of whom was condemned to suffer today, but the other is acquitted. Mr Thomas Sparrow said he thought the execution would be on the bridge before Billington's door, but I am happy to find this is not so. The arrest of these men has struck such a panic into the minds of the others that no less than four have fled.

An example had been made. We would be shocked today by the sharp and sudden revenge taken by the law, but there is no doubt that Wedgwood was well pleased with the way in which the riot had been handled. He wrote a pamphlet titled, 'Advice to the People of the Potteries', reminding them that thirty years earlier their homes had been 'miserable huts', whereas now they lived in 'mostly new and comfortable houses', earning 'near double their previous wages'. After reading this chapter you can decide for yourself whether Josiah's advice, to settle down and live lawfully, was sound or selfish.

WAGES

Certainly wages were much higher. Wedgwood's partner, Thomas Whieldon, had kept a record of the wages he paid, and he notes weekly payments of 8 shillings to a thrower and turner, 7s 6d to a handler, 5s 6d to an ovenman, 2s for a boy lathe-treader. Thirty years later Wedgwood's throwers earned 17s or 18s, his handlers 15s, and his ovenmen 12s. Prices had not risen anything like so quickly, so that these workers must have been better off. (Remember that this was 200 years ago when 18s was worth £10 or even £15 of our money today.)

Such increases in wages could be earned in the other rapidly growing industries – in cotton mills and coal mines, or iron foundries and furnaces. However, many workers at this time felt badly treated and bitterly hated the changes which brought them more money. Early factories and mills were often thought of as prisons.

Perhaps this was because the workers were not yet used to regular hours of work. Daniel Defoe had noticed that, 'There is nothing more frequent than for an Englishman to work until he had got his pockets full of money, and then go and be idle or perhaps drunk till 'tis all gone'. They preferred to work furiously for a few days and then relax in their own time. They felt that they could do what they wanted when they wanted.

The factories took away their freedom. An industrialist who had bought expensive machinery could not afford to let it 44 stand idle whilst 'hands' or workers enjoyed themselves. Orders of goods had to be delivered on time if the customer was to be satisfied. The workers had to be trained in the new *discipline* of the factory – just as schoolchildren have to learn the rules and discipline of a new school.

TRAINING

Wedgwood had much trouble in training his workers to be skilled and reliable. He could not win orders from famous or foreign customers unless he could promise good quality and swift delivery. However, most of his first workers were used to a casual, if not care-free, existence. Josiah had to make them more efficient if he was to succeed. One way in which he did this was by allowing each worker to specialise, or learn to become expert, in only one aspect of pottery manufacture. (See p. 31).

He also tried to make them more serious and responsible at work. His aim was 'to make such machines of the men as cannot *err*'. He could do this by either punishments or rewards. The final punishment was dismissal – and even skilled men were sacked, although Wedgwood hated to lose workers on whom he had spent time and money in training. In 1776 an artist and designer named Radford was told to leave Etruria because he could not keep regular hours and was setting a bad example to 'ten times better men than himself'.

The early factory-owners were keen to discipline and drill their workers into punctuality – arriving at work on time and leaving work on time. At Etruria a bell was rung to call the men to work. Josiah drew up detailed instructions for his porter, and these show clearly his eagerness to improve efficiency at Etruria. Here are parts of these instructions:

Business of a porter

Summer

Ring bell	5.45 a.m.
Chime bell	6 to 6.10 a.m. *Admonish* those who are not at work at that hour.
	6.20 a.m. Shut door till breakfast time,

take book around and check attendance.

8.30 a.m. Bell for breakfast.

9.00 a.m. A little before, bell for work again.

The porter might have a system of tickets to save himself going round the works, or a list of names in the lodge which he could mark with chalk. (This is an early attempt to start a clocking-in system.)

If working overtime, Ring bell at 6 to 6.30 for supper.

Winter

The first bell is to be quarter of an hour before they can see to work, and the last bell when they can no longer see.

A less drastic form of punishment than dismissal was the use of fines. Workers who disobeyed certain rules had fixed amounts stopped from their wages. These *forfeits* were quite heavy – they would be the equivalent of as much as £2 in today's money. Here is a list of the rules which were enforced at Etruria about 1780:

Any person seen throwing within the grounds of the manufactory, to forfeit 2/6d.

Any person leaving a fire in their rooms at night, to forfeit 2/6d.

Any workman leaving scraps in their rooms, so as to get dirty, to forfeit 2/6d.

Any workman striking or otherwise abusing an overlooker to lose his place.

Any workman bringing ale or liquor into the manufactory in working hours, to forfeit 2/6d.

Any person playing fives against any of the walls where there are windows, to forfeit 2/-.

At least most of the rules at Etruria were sensible and reasonable, not like the rule in one cotton mill which said, 'If any hand is seen talking to another, whistling, or singing, he will be fined sixpence.' Nevertheless workers do not like being told what they can and cannot do, even though the reasons may be sound – especially when they had never obeyed such rules before. Perhaps this is why the early factories were hated so bitterly.

Wedgwood was not completely successful in his struggle against the slackness of his workers. The lazy and drunken ones feared Josiah (he told Bentley, 'my name has been made a scarecrow to the workers'), but they forgot his rules, or ignored them, whenever they could. Even his best men took days off to go drinking. When Josiah was on honeymoon, all deliveries of his pottery stopped completely.

The workers loved to celebrate all the old religious festivals, glad of any excuse to escape from the weekly routine. These 'wakes' or holidays were always interfering with Wedgwood's plans and production. He wearily complained to Bentley, 'wakes must be observed, though the world was to end with them'. He kept this in mind in 1772, during a bad trading period, when he could justify closing his works with the argument that, 'the men can keep wake after wake in summer, when it is for their own convenience and pleasure, and they must now take a few holidays for our convenience'.

Generally, however, Wedgwood was a kind and careful employer who preferred to train his workers in good habits by rewards and encouragement rather than by punishments. The 'carrot' was better than the 'stick' – it brought better work and higher profits. Wedgwood therefore paid high wages, but tried to link wages with output by paying piece rates – a skilled worker was paid according to the pieces of pottery he helped to produce.

Josiah also tried to make the lives of his workers more pleasant when they were outside the factory. He took great interest in, and provided much money for, the schools and hospitals which they needed. He provided good houses for them to live in. Eventually both Wedgwood and the workers benefited, and the men whom Josiah had called 'idle, drunken and worthless' in 1770 had changed by 1790 into 'a very good sett of hands'.

Because Etruria was not near an existing town or village, Josiah had to build a completely new village for his workers. These new houses were not luxurious, but they were better than the cottages and hovels of earlier times. These had usually contained only one living room and one bedroom, and the dark low rooms probably smelt of stale food and cooking. Pigs and poultry were kept in the living room. The thatched roof, thick walls, rough beams and outside stairways must have made life in such cottages dismal and depressing.

Colliers' houses near Newcastle, 1778. Notice the outside staircases and the pig being driven out of doors

Wedgwood's houses were certainly much better. He began by building forty-two, in one long street from the canal bridge by the factory. They were roomy and well-lit, with windows with small panes of green glass, some with bulls' eyes. The front door steps were made of iron, six inches wide, and were kept beautifully polished. They were much bigger than the old cottages – having two storeys and two bed-rooms, with an inside staircase and hall, and a separate kitchen and living room downstairs. There was a passage way between every two houses, and land for a garden at the back. A water pump was provided for every dozen houses, and each house had its own outside toilet. By 1816 there were 111 houses and, by 1865, 190 in the village. Josiah also built bake-houses and ovens in which the workers could bake their bread at a charge of $\frac{1}{2}d$ per loaf. The rent paid for these houses was 1s 3d to 2s per week when they were first built.

Here is a detailed estimate for the complete building of two houses, sent by the local builder, Thomas Shaw, to Josiah. It is followed by the agreement or contract that they both eventually signed (see p. 109). From it you will see that a worker's house cost Josiah about £30 to build, so that he could recover the full cost, if his tenants paid their rents regularly, in ten years at the most. By contrast he estimated that his own home had cost more than £2,500 to build.

Estimate for two houses

Brick and workmanship	£20: 0: 0
Tiles and workmanship	7:19: 6
Floors and laying	1:13: 2
Plaister work	5:17: 6
Timber	10:11: 2
Workmanship at floors and roof	7:14: 7
Stairs	2: 4: 4
Doors and cases	2:16: 0
Windows	2:10: 6
Fireplace Barrs	4: 0
The two little houses (toilets)	2: 7: 0
	64: 5: 9
Sinking foundations and use of scaffold poles	14: 3
	£65: 0: 0

On these conditions I promise to build & complete two dwelling houses agreeable to the particulars of the Estimate N° 1 in this book in a good workmanlike manner for the sum of sixty five pounds paid to me by the J. J. Wedgwood when the houses are finished. All which is to be in four months from the date hereof on the penalty of forfeiting five pounds that is to say if they are not finished in that time then the undertaker is to receive sixty pounds only for the two houses, & it is further agreed that if there is any brick used in the walls which do not stand the weather that then the P. undertaker shall replace such brick at his own expence In witness of the above agreements we have hereunto set our hands the 30th of May 1769 — Josiah Wedgwood

Thos. Shaw.

Wedgwood's workers had to work such long hours that it is no wonder they looked forward eagerly to the holidays and week-ends. No doubt many of them drank heavily and gambled their wages away. Many of them probably still enjoyed sports which seem cruel and savage to us today. Bear-baiting and bull-baiting were still popular. Here is a description of bull-baiting:

> They tie a rope to the root of the horns of the bull, and fasten the other end to an iron ring fixed to a stake driven into the ground; so that this cord being about 15 feet long, the bull is confined to a sphere of about 30 feet diameter. Those that are desirous to exercise their dogs stand round about, and when the sport begins they let loose one of the dogs. The dog runs at the bull, the bull beats the ground with his feet, which he joins together as close as possible, his chief aim being not to gore the dog with the point of his horn (when the bull's horns are too sharp they put them into a kind of wooden sheath) but to slide one of them under the dog's belly and to throw him so high in the air that he may break his neck in the fall. This often happens.

To increase the enjoyment the bull or bear was beaten with clubs, and cats, monkeys, dogs and fireworks were sometimes tied to its tail and legs. Cock-fighting was another popular

Cockfighting – after William Hogarth's engraving. (The shadow is that of a man who had been 'basketed' above the arena for failing to pay his debts: he is offering his watch)

amusement. The pit was often behind an inn or even in the churchyard. Here is a description by a visiting Frenchman:

> They are large but short-legged birds, their feathers are scarce, they have no crests to speak of, and are very ugly to look at. The stage on which they fight is round and small. One of the cocks is released, and struts about proudly for a few seconds. He is then caught up and his enemy appears. When the bets are made, one of the cocks is placed on either end of the stage; they are armed with steel or silver spurs, and immediately rush at each other and fight furiously. They rarely give up until one of them is dead. The spectators are ordinarily composed of common people, and the noise is terrible, and it is impossible to hear yourself speak unless you shout.

Cruelty to animals was apparently commonplace. Another favourite 'sport' was goose-riding, which continued until well after 1800. Live geese were tied to a rope and dangled seven or eight feet from the ground with their necks well greased. The sport was to see if the competitors, riding ponies, could grab the birds by the neck and pull their heads off as they dashed past.

At the fairs and feasts there were other, less cruel, amusements. Tugs-of-war, climbing the greasy pole and foot-races all offered plenty of opportunity for fun and gambling. Boxing and wrestling were becoming organised, with certain rules and styles established. Cricket and football were also becoming rather more organised. Cricket was very popular; it was played in rough fields and even streets. There were two stumps six inches apart and a foot high, and bowling was always underhand. The bat was curved, and the players sometimes wore top hats and long coloured coats for serious games. Betting always took place on the result, and freak matches were arranged – eleven one-armed men against eleven one-legged men, for example.

Football was popular on Shrove Tuesdays, but it bore little resemblance to the modern game. Teams and goal-posts were 51

Cricket — notice the score-keeper with his tally

unnecessary – the ball was kicked by anybody, anywhere, and anyhow. A foreigner described it simply as 'a Useful, Charming Exercise. It is a Lether Ball about as Big as One's Hed, fill'd with Wind. This is kick'd about from one to t'uther in Streets by Him or Her that cann gette it. And that is all the Arte of it.'

There were less exciting games such as bowls. A game which has almost died out today was very popular then – Knur and Spell. Again heavy gambling accompanied this contest between players to see who could knock a piece of wood, shaped rather like a modern cricket bail, the furthest, with a delicately balanced striker.

Etruria was still far enough away from the towns for poaching to be possible, but the punishments for those caught were becoming so harsh that only those who were desperately hungry would risk it.

Another pleasure which could still be enjoyed by the poorer classes was that of open-air dancing. The old dances were remembered and passed on to children – hornpipes and morris dances especially.

Yet many of Wedgwood's workers were becoming less and less interested in drinking, gambling, dancing and sport. John Wesley's influence was strong in Staffordshire – and this open-

John Wesley

air preacher convinced the poor that they had their proper worth before God. He also convinced them that in order to be 'saved' they must live more sober and respectable lives. Thus the old savagery and brutality, the drunkenness and the gambling, were under attack from both Wesley's Methodist Church and Wedgwood's factory rules. Many of Josiah's workers began to go to chapel on Sundays instead of to the tavern.

8 Wedgwood the Businessman

Until 1764 Wedgwood had concentrated upon making useful pottery, but he had always been interested in increasing his sales of decorative or ornamental ware. In 1768 he developed a black pottery, with a rich smooth finish, in which beautiful vases were made. This became very popular, and still is today. Wedgwood was right when he told Bentley, 'the black is *sterling* and will last forever'.

'The black is sterling and will last forever'. Hedgehog bulb pot, mug and condiment set in the black 'basalt' ware

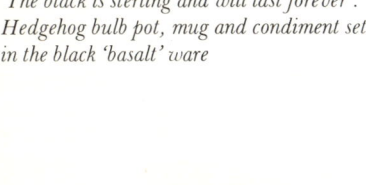

Blue and white early morning tea set in Jasper ware

Thomas Bentley was a partner who could spread Wedgwood's fame in the highest circles of London society. What was needed was a new type of decorative pottery which would make it easy for him to imitate the popular styles of ancient Greece and Rome. Wedgwood wanted a breakthrough in decorative pottery to match the great sales which Queen's Ware had brought him in useful ware.

In 1774, after thousands of experiments, Josiah at last succeeded. He perfected the making of 'Jasper' ware – the type of pottery which most people now think of when they hear the name of Wedgwood. This was described by Josiah as a 'white biscuit' pottery of 'exquisite beauty and delicacy', which would 'receive colours through its whole substance, in a manner which no other body, ancient or modern, has been known to do.' The coloured background (light or dark blue, green, yellow or lilac) provided a perfect contrast to the finely modelled white decorations which were applied by hand – each figure of the projecting *relief* was separately fixed, its details kept clear and sharp by a skilled ornamenter. Round the edges were repeating patterns of flower, leaf and plant designs. Indeed the pale blue type of jasper became so famous and popular that people now talk of 'Wedgwood Blue'. The ware was very difficult to fire and Josiah invented a more efficient thermometer for measuring very high temperatures. In 1783 he was elected a Fellow of the Royal Society, a famous group of scientists, in appreciation of this *pyrometer*.

There were many things for which the new ware could be used. It could be both useful – for cups, saucers, jugs, bowls, tea-pots; and ornamental – for vases and furniture inlays. In time Jasper was used for all kinds of articles, such as buttons, snuff boxes, beads, sword belts, paint boxes, combs, chess-sets, coach panels, rings, door handles, desks and opera glasses.

Wedgwood could now produce many different types of pottery at Etruria. However, trade secrets were very difficult to keep in Staffordshire and every improvement was quickly copied. By 1784 there were twenty-five potters in Burslem alone

A piece from a Jasper Chess set: the King

Jasper's many uses:
scent bottle, brooches, comb and necklace

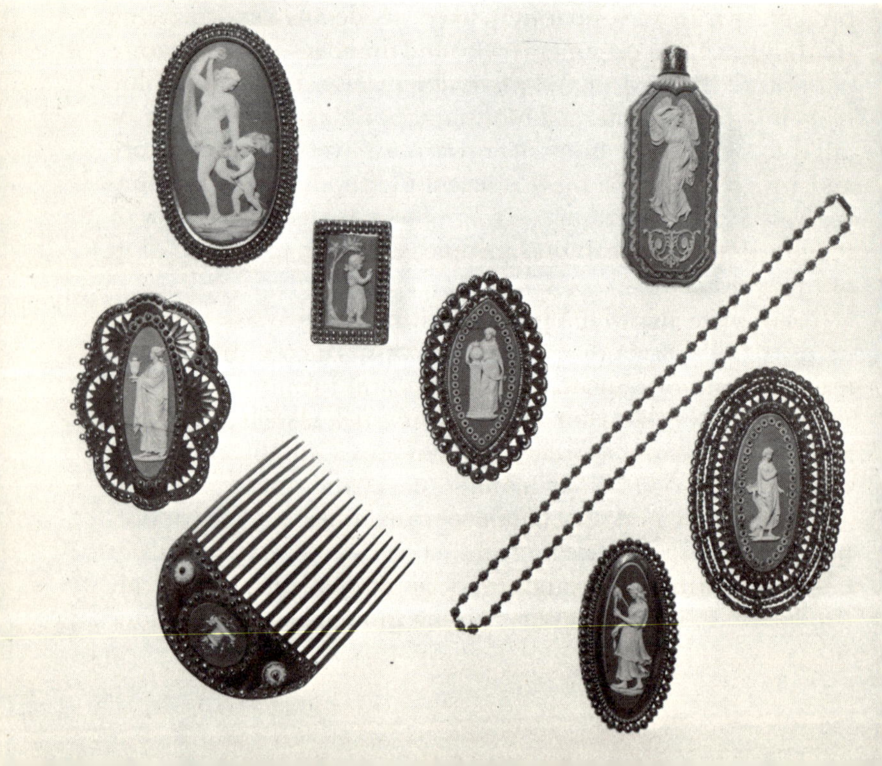

making the new type of cream ware, and selling it. At Leeds much beautiful creamware was made more cheaply than Wedgwood's. Other famous potters such as Spode, Palmer and Adams made Jasper ware which many people consider to be even more beautiful than Josiah's – and again they sold it more cheaply.

Why then was it Wedgwood who captured the greatest share of the growing market for pottery, despite his high prices? To explain this we must look closely at the business ability of Wedgwood and Bentley, and at the methods which they used to sell their pottery.

THE APPEAL TO THE NOBILITY

Wedgwood and Bentley believed very strongly in the value of 'snob appeal' as an aid in selling their pottery. They thought that if the nobility could be persuaded to buy from them, the middle classes would quickly follow their example. Naturally therefore Josiah was delighted to obtain the custom of the royal family. In 1771 he told Bentley, 'Their majesties are very good indeed! I hope we shall not lose their favour.'

Bentley was extremely useful to Josiah in this respect, for since he was popular and accepted in all the best circles he could persuade the rich to buy from Wedgwood. Josiah clearly understood this for he wrote to Bentley: 'Be so good as to let me know what is going on in the great world. How many lords and dukes visit your rooms, praise your beauties, thin your shelves and fill your purses.'

Josiah was determined not to let anything interfere with this favour from the great. He refused to allow common folk to enter his London show room because he did not want the nobility to be either embarrased or annoyed, for he knew that his 'present sett of customers would not mix with the rest of the world'.

Wherever the rich and famous flocked together, Wedgwood wanted his pottery to be seen and talked about. The spa water at Bath attracted many nobles who wanted a change from London or from the country. Josiah quickly opened a show-

Bath, where Wedgwood opened a shop

room there. The Irish nobility were tempted by a shop in Dublin. Again, however, the tone of the sales approach was to be dignified. When Josiah's agent, Mr Ward, began to use 'common' methods to advertise his pottery, delivering hand bills in the Pump Room (where the water was drunk), he was quickly ordered to stop doing so. As Josiah said: 'We have always appeared in a very different light to common shopkeepers, but this step (in my opinion) will sink us exceedingly.'

SPECIAL ORDERS

The nobility sometimes ordered individual services from Josiah. These were called 'uniques', as only one of the kind was

A plate from the Frog service

made. These orders were often a worry and they took up a great deal of time – but Josiah did not like to refuse them. The most famous order came from Catherine the Great, the Empress of Russia, in 1772. She wanted a table service of 1,282 pieces – she must have been expecting many guests. It was called the 'Frog Service' as each piece had a green frog painted on it, and when it was finished in 1773 it had 1,244 separate hand paintings of the country houses of the English nobility.

The order brought Josiah fame – and profit. The final price was £3,500, and he made £2,000 on the service. Yet it also brought him a problem which illustrates again his fear of losing the favour of the nobility. The difficulty was to decide which country houses to paint on which pieces. Josiah did not wish to offend anyone, but as all the nobles were eager to have their mansions on the largest pieces, not everyone could be satisfied, for, as Josiah sadly remarked, 'There are more noble lords than *tureens*'.

He also worried about whether to show the Frog Service in London before it was sent to St Petersburg. Eventually his pride won and he did display it, but not until he had thought very carefully about the matter. As he told Bentley:

> On the one side, the exhibition will bring an immense number of people of fashion into our rooms, but you see the danger. For suppose a gentleman thinks himself neglected, either by the omission of his house, or by putting it on a small plate, he then becomes our enemy.

THE LONDON SHOWROOM

Wedgwood was very proud of his London showroom. Here is a picture of it – notice the large room with the tables set with services and the cases filled with vases. Well-dressed customers are chatting and inspecting the pottery.

One of Josiah's letters to Bentley is worth careful reading as it shows his great attention to detail. Wedgwood obviously appreciated the importance of presenting his pottery attractively – what modern salesmen would call 'window dressing' or 'packaging'. Wedgwood carefully explained his reasons

Wedgwood's London showroom

'for wanting A LARGE ROOM IN LONDON'. This was 'to enable me to show various Table and dessert services, six or eight at least; such services must be shown in order to do the needfull with the Ladys in the neatest, genteelest and best method'. Josiah recommended that the arrangements of pottery should be altered every few days, 'to make the whole a new scene, even to the same Company, every time they shall bring their friends to visit us'.

Wedgwood reported on the success of such methods:

> The two first days after the alteration we sold three complete sets of Vases at 2 or 3 Guineas a set, besides many pairs of them, which vases had been in my rooms for 6 to 8 and some of them 12 months, and wanted nothing but arrangement to sell them. And besides room for my ware, I must have more room for my Ladys, for they sometimes come in very large *shoals* together, and one party are often obliged to wait until another have done their business.

KEEPING UP WITH CHANGING TASTES

Wedgwood's pleasant showroom became a fashionable meeting place for the nobility in the 1780s, a place where gossip could be exchanged at the same time as pottery was bought. Josiah was naturally flattered and delighted, but he did not relax. He knew that fashions could change and that snob appeal had to be linked firmly with the latest fashion. Thomas Bentley therefore had to make sure that Josiah's pottery kept in touch with changing tastes. It was Bentley who warned Wedgwood that decorations in gold paint (gilding) were becoming unpopular, so that Wedgwood quickly dismissed his gilders.

Bentley knew that the art of ancient Greece and Rome was extremely popular and advised Wedgwood to set to work to satisfy this craze for the 'antique or classical'. Even ruined columns were made (as you can see in the bottom righthand corner of the picture of the showroom). Greek vases were copied as closely as possible, although not always in every detail because the originals had naked figures which might

The Portland Vase

A skilled craftsman in the late nineteenth century perfecting the jasper reliefs on a Portland vase

have made Wedgwood's genteel lady customers blush. Josiah therefore ordered his artists to clothe such figures in flowing gowns or fig leaves.

The most famous imitation, which brought Wedgwood as much fame as the Frog Service, was the Portland Vase. This was a copy of a Greek vase brought to England in 1780 and bought by the Duchess of Portland in 1785. Josiah succeeded in borrowing the vase and spent a great deal of time, money and effort in making an almost perfect copy in Jasper in 1789. This was Josiah's most famous single work, and is now used as a trade mark by the Wedgwood company. One of the first copies was sold for over £3,000 in 1964.

Bentley noticed that fashionable ladies were very proud of the whiteness of their hands. He therefore advised Josiah to make black tea-pots to bring out this whiteness clearly. Josiah was thus given a useful sale in 1772 which was a bad year, as we shall see later. He wrote gratefully to Bentley, 'Thanks for your discovery in favour of black tea-pots. I hope white hands will continue in fashion and then we may continue to make black tea-pots until you can find us better employment.'

Wedgwood employed famous artists to design for him. They included William Blake and George Stubbs, but the two most used were John Flaxman and William Hackwood. Flaxman went to Rome and sent back from there drawings of statues and monuments for Wedgwood. He was famous for his designs of ancient Greek gods and goddesses, but also for more homely scenes such as farming tasks, and children at play: skipping, rolling marbles, playing hide and seek. Hackwood was well known for his portraits of famous men and women from past and present. Their work was very popular, and helped Wedgwood to increase his sales of Jasper ware.

PRICES
In general Josiah did not worry very much about what prices to charge for his pottery. He usually allowed Thomas Bentley in London to charge as much as he could possibly obtain for the vases and ornamental ware. Wedgwood's usual method was to 67

combine high quality with high prices (although he would sometimes reduce a price in order to sell to his beloved nobility. In 1769 he told Bentley, 'I think what you charge 34/- for should be a Guinea and a half – 34 is so odd a sum that there is no paying it genteely'.)

However, in 1771 there began a general drop in sales. Wedgwood told Bentley gloomily: 'The general trade seems to be going to ruin on the gallop. Large stocks remain in London and in the country, and there is little demand. The Potters are quite in a Pannick for their trade.' The ways in which Josiah dealt with this threat show how he could change his prices to fit changing times.

He decided first of all to make a thorough investigation of all the costs involved in making his pottery, so that he could reduce his prices slightly if possible. As he told Bentley, 'the problem is not to fix the prices so high as to prevent sale, nor so low as to prevent profitt upon them.' One result of this survey was that he found that he was charging far too much for the large pieces. For three sizes of candlestick he calculated that:

The 9″ size cost 4/10¾d to make and sold at 12/–
The 12″ size cost 5/7¼d to make and sold at 27/–
The 14″ size cost 7/11½d to make and sold at 45/–

He therefore told Bentley to reduce the prices, 'because we have advanced the prices by the inches out of all proportion to the real expense'.

Wedgwood was even more worried when he found out that his actual profits were nothing like as great as his calculations told him they should be. He took into account the costs of raw materials, wages, fuel, rent, transport, losses and breakages, and selling charges. Even so he thought that he should be making twice as much money as he appeared to be.

He quickly found out the reason, and equally quickly put it right. He discovered that his chief clerk in London, Ben Mather, was dishonest and lazy, and that he was living a life of extravagance, 'far beyond anything he earns from us (in a lawful way) would support'. Josiah dared not dismiss Mather immediately, as this would allow the clerk to go and collect thousands of pounds from customers who still owed money, and had not yet learnt of his dismissal. He decided to ask Bentley to send Mather away on an errand for a week to Bath, which would give them time to re-organise the London shop and find how much the clerk had pocketed. When Mather did return he was not sacked – another example of Josiah's generosity – but given a less important job. Eight years later, however, he was dismissed when it was found that he had been cheating again.

Josiah insisted in future that the clerks in London had to send their records of sales every week to Etruria by Monday's post. Debts had to be collected much more regularly. Eventually his calculations of expected profits began to appear more realistic.

Nevertheless, the general trade did not recover quickly, and Josiah was afraid that he might have to sack some of the workers at Etruria. He avoided this, however, by trying to sell to a different type of customer at slightly lower prices. The pottery which he had sold to the upper classes at high prices by appealing to their sense of snobbery, fashion and high quality he now decided to sell to the 'middling classes'. His letter to Bentley during the crisis, on 23 August 1772, explains this clearly and provides a good summary of Josiah's attitude to prices:

> The Great People have now had my vases in their Palaces long enough for them to be seen and admired by the Middling classes of people. Although a great price was at first necessary in order to make the Vases *esteemed* ornaments for Palaces, that reason no longer exists. Their fame is established, and the Middling People would probably buy huge quantities at reduced prices.

INCREASING THE SPEED OF PRODUCTION

Reducing prices meant lower profits, and Josiah certainly did not like the idea of that.

His investigation into costs gave him the clue to the way in which he could reduce prices and preserve high profits. Although there appeared to be little he could do on the 'useful' side to save time and work, unless he was willing to make bad quality pottery, there was the chance to cut down on the costs of production of ornamental pottery.

Josiah realised that a large part of the cost of each vase was made up of fixed costs such as rent, wages, fuel, machinery – and he also saw that these fixed costs remained the same whatever the number of vases made. He therefore determined to make 'the greatest quantity possible in a given time' so that the fixed costs would be spread over more articles, and the selling price could be lowered so that more customers would buy. He decided to spur his workers into faster production by reducing the pay they received for each piece but making it possible for them to increase their output and still earn the same wages as before. He explained all this carefully and clearly to Bentley in a letter of 23 August 1772:

> You will see the vast importance in most manufactures of making the greatest quantity possible in a given time. Rent goes on whether we make much or little. Wages to the Boys and Odd (Job) Men, Warehouse Men and Bookkeeper, who are a kind of satellite to the makers (Throwers, Turners etc.) are nearly the same whether we make twenty dozen of vases or ten dozen per week. The same may be said of most of the incidental expenses. Coals for the workshop fire must be increased rather than lessened when the men are idle, in order to keep them warm. The cost of modelling and moulds, and the expense of sale, would not be much increased if we could sell double the quantity at our Rooms in Town, which lowering some of the prices may enable us to do.

Wedgwood was successful. With prices only slightly reduced, and still well above those of other potters, he was able to sell to a larger middle-class market and avoid huge losses. When prosperity did return in 1774 Josiah was quick to raise his prices again, but the lower prices, combined with his *reputation* for quality and his instinct for fashion, had enabled him to stay in business at a time when many other potters lost all their money.

The slump also impressed upon Wedgwood the importance of exporting pottery to foreign customers. Once again Bentley was a great help, for he could tell Josiah what kinds of pottery different countries preferred. Bentley knew that most Americans were not yet ready to buy very expensive things; he knew that the Russians liked vivid, colourful pottery; that the Venetians liked to drink coffee out of small cups. Bentley could translate Wedgwood's catalogues (lists of goods and prices) into foreign languages. He could persuade English ambassadors at foreign courts to buy Wedgwood's pottery, so that these distinguished travellers spread Wedgwood's fame.

Until 1770 the Staffordshire potters had sold their wares to English merchants at Liverpool, Hull, London or Bristol. These merchants then sold the pottery abroad for as much profit as they could. Josiah wanted to do without these 'middle men', and began to deal directly with the foreigners himself. Unfortunately the foreign agents or buyers were not always honest – quite often they sold Wedgwood's pottery but did not bother to send him any money in return. Wedgwood soon grew tired of this and insisted on cash before delivery. One very good and reliable agent was a Mr Van Veldhuysen in Amsterdam. Wedgwood told Bentley in 1772, 'Mr Veldhuysen is to buy and pay for the ware in Amsterdam before it is delivered to him, so there is no risk.' Six years later Josiah was very happy with the arrangement, for he reported to Bentley on 4 November 1778:

We have a pretty good order this week from Amsterdam, consisting of 10 busts of 12″ and 5″, 70 or 80 heads framed, 9 dozen flower pots, 20 dozen tea-pots and other things in black. I am told Veldhuysen's warehouse is fitted up very elegantly and believe he is likely to do very well both for himself and us.

Ten years later this partnership was still flourishing, for on 22 April 1788, Wedgwood received the following order from Amsterdam for 'various goods which we expect very soon. We hope they will be packed carefully':

Blue Bordered Ware
10 doz. 2nd size Oval and Salad Plates
  6 doz. Oval dishes 19 inches
    2 doz.   ,,   ,,   20 ,,
    2 doz.   ,,   ,,   18 ,,
    6 doz.   ,,   ,,   17 ,,
    8 doz.   ,,   ,,   16 ,,
  10 doz.   ,,   ,,   15 ,,
  10 doz.   ,,   ,,   14 ,,
  10 doz.   ,,   ,,   13 ,,
  12 doz.   ,,   ,,   12 ,,
  4 doz. cups
  4 doz. strawberry dishes
& stands
  4 doz. round dishes 19 inches
    2 doz.   ,,   ,,   18 ,,

Queen's Ware
10 Crates flatt plates

  4 crates soup bowls
  4 crates round dishes
  6 doz. hand basins, round rims
  6 doz. hand basins, flatt rims
  6 doz. Water *Ewers*, 3rd si.
  4 doz. Cups
10 doz. Round twig baskets and stands
  6 doz. *octagonal* strawberry dishes, and stands.
  6 doz. beaded strawberry dishes, and stands.
(largest size)

Blue and White Jasper, with reliefs.
1 Vase No. 279 9″ £2:11: 6
1 Vase No. 296 8″ 2: 2: 0
2 Vases No. 276 6″ 3: 0: 0
1 Vase No. 276 10″ 2: 2: 0
2 Vases No. 280 8″ 3: 3: 0
2 Vases No. 282 7″ 2: 2: 0

Three black seals, nos. 23, 32, 25.
3 doz. round fluted black teapots.
6 *Ecritoires*, with sand boxe and holes to hold candles.

By 1780 Wedgwood sent most of his pottery abroad – to cities like St Petersburg, Naples, Leipzig, Paris, Venice and New York. He told a Member of Parliament that, 'the bulk of our manufactures are exported to foreign markets, for our home *consumption* is trifling in comparison to what we send abroad. The principal of these markets are the Continents and Islands of North America.'

Although Wedgwood was careful to avoid sales methods which might make his pottery appear vulgar, he did think that increased personal contacts could bring him customers. In 1777 a John Brownbill was employed as a traveller, but he was not very efficient and he was soon replaced by Josiah's nephew, Thomas Byerley (who helped teach Wedgwood's children). Byerley did much better, travelling round the country collecting old debts and finding new customers. He later went on a tour of Europe, taking the Portland Vase to exhibit in Amsterdam, Hanover, Frankfurt and Berlin, in an attempt to spread the fame of Wedgwood ware.

PAID CARRIAGE: SATISFACTION OR MONEY BACK

The final example of Wedgwood's skill as a businessman comes from the attention which he paid to the distribution and delivery of his goods. Although the transport of pottery was expensive, and many breakages occurred, Wedgwood's very high prices and profits allowed him to offer free delivery.

As early as 1769 he had sent his pottery free of charge to London. The constant complaints from his customers about breakages gave him an even better idea. An American, John Wanamaker, is often said to have been the first to offer a 'Satisfaction or Money back' Guarantee, but it was Josiah Wedgwood's policy one hundred years earlier. Here is an extract from one of Josiah's advertisements in 1771:

> Mr Wedgwood *engages* that every piece shall be delivered whole at their houses in any part of England, or if any of the goods are broke, the deficiency shall be made up either in goods or by deducting so much from the bill, at the *option* of the purchaser, who shall likewise be at liberty to return the whole, or any part of the goods they ordered (paying the carriage back), if they do not find them agreeable to their wishes.

This appears to be a very generous offer, but Josiah knew that he was not really risking very much. However, as he shrewdly 73 observed to Bentley, it would encourage people to buy from him:

> at present my customers do return their goods if they do not like them, and they are out of humour if the breakages are not made up to them in some way or another, but this advertisement will tell thousands who at present know nothing of it, that they run no risk at all (except a little payment of the carriage back) by ordering goods from me, and I make no doubt it will encourage many to order services who, without such information, would not think of doing so.

Thus Josiah Wedgwood backed up his improvements in pottery by an extremely skilful sense of business. Helped by Thomas Bentley, he had secured a safe upper class custom. Bentley died in 1780, but by then Wedgwood's name was firmly established. In times of bad trade he had tried to extend his sales to the middle classes. In 1777 he had expressed his aim clearly, telling Bentley: 'Few Ladies dare buy anything out of the common style 'til *authoris'd* by their betters – by the Ladies of superior spirit who set the tone.'

No detail was too unimportant for Wedgwood to study, and he was prepared to scheme and work to increase his sales both at home and abroad. In the next chapter you can read more about the kind of lives led by Wedgwood's customers in England, and in the final chapter you can find out something about Josiah's wider interests in transport and politics.

9 Wedgwood's Customers

THE NOBILITY

Although Wedgwood could not sell vast quantities of pottery to the nobility because there were so few of them, he clearly recognised the very great influence of this small class. The greatest of them – families such as the Devonshires, the Bedfords, the Newcastles and the Rockinghams – owned over 100,000 acres of land (whole counties, sometimes) and were richer than many European kings.

Sometimes they misused their power. The Earl of Lincoln, who was rather ashamed of his fatness, had an apprentice boy beaten to death for 'gazing at him in the street'. When the Duke of Somerset travelled, he sent servants ahead to clear the roads and stop people staring at him as he passed. One farmer refused to be stopped from looking over his own hedge and held up his pig, 'so that it should see him too'.

Such cruel and proud behaviour was becoming rare. Although the English nobility liked to keep their distance (as in Wedgwood's showroom), they usually managed to mix more easily with the rest of society than did the nobility of other countries. In another book in this series, 'The French Revolution', you can read about the way in which the behaviour of the French nobility helped to bring bloodshed and terror. In England there was a great deal of misery and unrest, but no revolution. One reason for this is that through contact with other classes the English nobility sometimes won respect and even affection. The Duke of Dorset played cricket in the same team as his gardener. Wedgwood and other businessmen realised that such easy relations gave the nobility a strong influence over other customers.

Rich living by the nobility: the dining room at Luton Hoo, Bedfordshire

Bloomsbury Square with Bedford House. Only the richest of the nobility could afford such splendid London mansions

THE COUNTRY HOUSE

The richest nobles built magnificent houses on their lands. This house was a proof of their wealth and power. The gardens alone at the Duke of Marlborough's palace at Blenheim had cost £500,000. Places such as Castle Howard in Yorkshire, Chatsworth in Derbyshire or Woburn in Bedfordshire were a constant reminder of the power and wealth of the nobility who lived in them.

These houses were not built just for show. They were the central meeting place of the whole family, both now and in the future, for these nobles built for their children's children. Huge houses were needed to entertain the endless stream of guests. Lord Hervey's social life was rather quiet, yet he wrote: 'We used to sit down to dinner a snug little party of about thirty odd, up to the chin in venison, beef, turkeys etc; and generally over the chin in claret, strong beer and punch.'

THE LONDON SEASON

The richest nobles spent part of every year in London. They sometimes had a house built there, such as Bedford House, which filled the north side of Bloomsbury Square. Many of them rented houses for the whole family. The ladies would keep up with the latest fashions – often visiting Wedgwood's showroom of course. At dances they would try to find suitable husbands for their daughters. The Lords visited coffee houses to talk about the latest news, went to gambling clubs, met their lawyers and discussed business.

INDUSTRY AND TRADE

If they had lived in France such lords would have had little business to discuss. Such matters were regarded there as not worth their attention. In England the nobles were always eager to increase their fortunes, so that they were often involved in trading companies and they often encouraged new ideas and inventions in industry. They were keen to mine the coal, iron, tin or lead which they found on their lands. They were interested in improving transport by road, river or canal. They quickly realised the profits to be made out of buying and selling

Young nobles on a grand tour, visiting the Uffizi Gallery in Florence

houses and land. Naturally they were not always successful – the Duke of Chandos put money into a scheme for oyster pearl fishing off Anglesey, which even he later admitted was 'most ridiculous'. The nobles usually, however, filled their pockets more often than they burnt their fingers.

THE GRAND TOUR

Another expensive habit enjoyed by the nobility was the Grand Tour. The rich sent their eldest sons on a tour of Europe which lasted from three to five years and cost thousands of pounds. It was sometimes so expensive that younger brothers had to make do with three years at Oxford or Cambridge, followed perhaps by a term at a foreign university.

On the tour, the eighteen – or nineteen-year old 'milord' would spend months in France and Italy, and sometimes also visit the Netherlands, Germany and Austria. He would scatter guineas wherever he went, picking up in return a smattering of foreign languages, a knowledge of art and architecture, useful skills such as fencing and horsemanship, and of course elegance in the drawing-room and the ball-room. You can read more about this in another book in this series – 'The Eighteenth-century Grand Tour.'

MANNERS

Unfortunately this elegance did not usually last very long. The English nobility were often rowdy or rude, behaving in a way which would shock us today. Horace Walpole tells how, for a guinea bet, Lord Cobham spat into Lord Hervey's hat, whilst Hervey was talking, hat in hand, with some ladies. Lord Manchester, our Ambassador in Paris, was criticised for blowing his nose into his napkin, and spitting in the middle of the room.

Such bad habits were slowly dying out, as the rules of better behaviour were being made and kept. Lord Chesterfield's careful letters of advice to his son show that good manners were becoming more and more important. At least Chesterfield could clearly explain what not to do:

> When an awkward fellow first comes into the room it is highly probable that his sword gets between his legs and throws him down. If he drinks tea or coffee, he scalds his mouth, lets either his cup or saucer fall and spills his tea or coffee on his breeches. When he drinks he always coughs in his glass and besprinkles the company.

CLOTHES

In the early eighteenth century the dress of the nobility had been extravagant in both style and cost. By 1780 the nobles who used Wedgwood's table services were more restrained in their clothes as well as their manners. One young nobleman paid 500 guineas for a suit in 1750. Another young dandy, who committed suicide when only thirty-two, left a wardrobe of clothes which was sold for £15,000 at an auction.

The men dressed in silk or satin coats, silk waistcoats, knee breeches and white frilly shirts. Colours were very bright – 79

A dandy in the 1780s. Note his complicated cosmetics

yellows, oranges, scarlets, blues and pinks – but these shades were replaced by quieter ones later. Some young people started a fashion for untidy clothes. They called themselves 'the Slovens' and wore wide hats with floppy brims, left their breeches unbuckled at the knee, and sometimes even left curling papers in their hair.

Expensive wigs were worn by men and women. Sir Robert Walpole spent more in one year on wigs than he paid wages to one of his footmen. Women wore such huge wigs that they began to look top heavy. The great change in women's clothes was the introduction from France of the hooped skirt. Hooded cloaks also became popular and the hoods were sometimes used to conceal notes from lovers.

A lady in riding dress and another in court dress (1778)

A Lady having her hair dressed

GAMBLING

Gambling was the great hobby of both rich and poor, but it was the rich who really devoted themselves to it. Coffee houses, such as the Cocoa Tree, Boodle's and White's, became gambling clubs where the nobility were prepared to gamble on anything – from how long a certain bishop might live, to whether such a duchess was likely to have children. *Wagers* were sacred – at one club, when a member collapsed bets were quickly made as to whether he would recover. Those with their money on his likely death complained that it was unfair to call a doctor. Perhaps the strangest bet of all was reported in 'The Times' in 1788: 'His Grace the Duke of Bedford has bet Lord Barrymore that the latter will not be able to eat a live cat for fifty guineas.'

EXTRAVAGANCE

The richest noblemen could afford to lose huge sums at the card table, and gambling was only one of many pleasures. The Duke of Chandos kept an orchestra of twenty-seven musicians at a cost of over £1,600 a year. We have seen that fortunes were spent on gardens and houses, but the craze for the old and antique led to a great liking for ruins. Those who did not possess them therefore had their own built. France and Italy were ransacked by the English nobility, who spent fortunes on paintings and sculptures to decorate their homes.

WHERE THE MONEY CAME FROM

Most of the money which paid for the house, the travel, the art treasures and the pleasures of the gaming and dinner tables came from the land. Rents and farm profits still provided the bulk of the income of the nobility. This income was pleasantly increased, however, by trade and industrial interests, and by the profits from politics.

When he returned from the Grand Tour, a young lord was not expected to live in idleness. Great possessions brought with them important duties; since the nobility owned so much of the land it was thought only right that they should run the country. The rewards of this service and duty were extremely great. Serving king and country enabled the nobility to serve themselves as well. Many a family's fortune was made, or restored, by the salaries, bribes and pensions brought by power in London. The Walpoles in the 1690s were only country gentlemen from Norfolk. After Sir Robert Walpole's long period of political power the family was one of the richest in England – rich enough for his youngest son, Horace, to do nothing except live in luxury, watching and writing about the habits of his countrymen at the new house he had built for himself in the latest fashion.

POLITICS
Sometimes the nobles used their power to persuade members of parliament to pass laws which appear selfish today – protecting farmers' profits and hunting rights. Any attack on private property was regarded with horror and stamped out with violence. Pickpockets who stole more than a shilling could be hung; indeed, the number of crimes punishable by death increased from about fifty in 1700 to two hundred by 1800. The poor were warned of the results of robbery by carcasses hanging at crossroads and heads rotting on spikes in London.

Usually, however, the nobles used their influence sensibly. If the country needed money for war, they were prepared to tax themselves – whereas in France the right not to pay taxes was seen as one of the things which made a man noble. In England the nobility encouraged new ideas about farming and industry. They allowed people to worship in whichever Church they chose to. Naturally the nobility looked after themselves when possible – but they did realise that, if they wanted to keep their wealth and power, they had also to try to look after other people too.

It was therefore the great nobility, helped by their poorer relations, the country gentlemen, who kept order throughout the land. Very often they appointed Justices of the Peace, who passed sentence on those who broke the law. Such men led a bewildering busy life, for they were responsible for the normal working of society. They had to check the weights and measures used by shopkeepers, and the prices which they charged. They had to give permission, by issuing licences, to men who wanted to run alehouses. They supervised the repair of roads and bridges. They were the men who looked after the upkeep of the very old, or very poor. Behind these Justices of the Peace was the power and influence of the great nobility. This is what Edmund Burke meant when he compared the nobles to 'the great Oaks that shade a country'.

THE MIDDLE CLASSES

The more numerous 'middling people' were usually serious, sober and respectable – they had to be. Josiah Wedgwood quickly saw that these classes could provide him with far more customers than the nobility which they loved to imitate, for although the merchants, shopkeepers, manufacturers, doctors and lawyers were becoming more and more important, they still followed the nobility closely in matters of style.

This was noticed in 1767 by Soames Jenkyns, who wrote: 'The merchant *vies* all the time with the first of our nobility, in his house, table and furniture. The Shopkeeper, who used to be well contented with one dish of meat, one fire and one maid, has now two or three times as many of each; his wife has her tea, her card-parties, and her dressing-room.' Even self-made manufacturers eagerly copied the nobility. When Sir Richard Arkwright was made High Sheriff of Derbyshire in 1787 he was very flattered and showed his fitness for the position (usually given to a nobleman) by appearing in public accompanied by thirty javelin men on black horses, and trumpeters dressed in scarlet and gold, mounted on grey horses. Another business-man, Jedediah Strutt, bought his son a copy of Lord Chester-field's advice, underlining certain passages for special attention. As he told his boy: 'It is almost as necessary to learn genteel be-haviour and a polite manner as it is to learn to speak, read or write.'

Although the middle classes were fascinated by the nobility they were already beginning to challenge their power. If the

'The fruits of early Industry and Economy' by George Morland. Note the rewards (expensive clothes, negro servant, comfortable house.) This merchant still appears to listen carefully to his clerk

nobles were all important in the country, it was the middle classes who were beginning to control the newly developing industrial towns. They were the leaders in places like Leeds, Manchester, Liverpool, Birmingham and Bradford. Men like Josiah Wedgwood were beginning to realise that if they acted together they could play a more important part in the government of England. Wedgwood organised an early example of such action – the General Chamber of Manufacturers in 1785. The manufacturers combined to put pressure on parliament to protect their industries by taxing the imports of goods from other countries, especially Ireland. Although the Chamber did not stay in existence for very long it did succeed in its immediate aim – the changes in taxation were made, the profits continued. Another example of the way in which the middle classes were working together is the development of 'Improvement Committees' in the large cities – the things to be improved being practical problems such as lighting, drainage and roads.

The world was a serious place for men like Wedgwood, Arkwright and Strutt. They thought that hard work was essential for success, but they were prepared to run risks in order to increase their profits. Gradually they developed their own attitudes and habits and began to forget or ignore the older way of life of the nobility. They encouraged people to save instead of to spend; they wanted new schools for their children which did not teach only Latin and Greek, like the old grammar and public schools, but modern, useful languages and science. They often disliked the old Church of England, the great support of the nobility, and worshipped in plainer, simpler chapels. They were eager to improve their own minds, and formed subscription libraries at which members paid small sums every week, which were used to buy books. They started debating societies at which serious topics could be discussed.

As they became increasingly wealthy they could afford to buy luxuries such as pottery. Josiah Wedgwood was quick to take advantage of their tastes. No subject which might appeal to his customers was missed if it was at all possible to give it expression in pottery. Heroes like Joseph Priestley the chemist, John

Wesley the preacher, and Captain Cook the discoverer were obvious subjects for jasper portraits. Nelson's great victory over the French in 1798 was quickly followed by a medallion. Any chance to increase sales was eagerly seized, as Wedgwood was shrewd enough to be able to make pottery which appealed to both the old nobility and the middle classes.

Jasper Medallion of Lord Nelson in 1798. Wedgwood was always quick to honour England's heroes – and at the same time increase his sales

10 Turnpikes, Canals, Ships

Josiah Wedgwood was a proud member of the 'Lunar Society' of Birmingham, one of the most famous of the new middle-class debating and discussion groups. They called themselves the 'Lunar Society' because they had to meet when the moon was full, so that they could see to travel home safely. The roads round Birmingham were so bad that they dare not travel on them when it was dark.

If you read the diaries or letters of people who lived at this time you will find endless complaints about the roads. John Wesley, who travelled all over England to preach to his followers, told how his horse once stumbled into a pot-hole so deep that both horse and man were nearly drowned. Arthur Young in 1770 gloomily described 'the infernall road between Wigan and Preston . . . with Ruts four feet deep', and warned 'all travelling to avoid this terrible County as they would the Divell, for a thousand to one they break their Necks or their Limbs by overthrowings or Breakings-Down'.

Such roads were annoying to the ordinary traveller, but to the businessman or farmer they could be disastrously expensive. Wedgwood used tons of coal, clay from Cornwall, salt and flint-stone – raw materials which were all made dearer by transport costs. Josiah calculated that he was paying eight shillings a ton for coal, of which six shillings was the cost of carrying it to his works. We have seen earlier that he was offering free delivery of finished pottery, and he was naturally eager to cut this expense down. In fact it was largely the high transport costs which had kept the Staffordshire pottery industry merely local until Wedgwood's time.

Road travel was not very comfortable, even on a busy road like the one from London to Dover

One cause of bad roads was the fact that their repair was usually the responsibility of each parish or village, so that only short stretches of road were very occasionally repaired by unwilling, unpaid and unskilled workers. Those who most desperately wanted better roads realised they would have to do something about it themselves. They formed Turnpike Trusts – that is groups of men agreed to ask Parliament to allow them to repair a certain stretch of road. To pay for this upkeep they charged *tolls* to those who used the roads, erecting turnpikes (gates with spikes on them) and toll houses at intervals on the improved road.

These turnpike trusts were not new, for the first was formed in 1663. After 1750, however, they were becoming much more common. The prices charged by the trusts varied, but usually they were 3*d* for every coach horse, 4*d* for each horse pulling a heavy wagon, 1*d* for a single horse and rider, 10*d* per score for cattle and 5*d* per score for sheep. Why do you think the prices were different?

Turnpike roads were usually much better than the old parish roads. Merchants and businessmen found them cheaper, despite the tolls, for carriages could carry heavy loads and still travel more quickly. These trusts also improved the methods of road building by employing skilled engineers such as John Metcalf, Thomas Telford and John Macadam.

Josiah Wedgwood was the leader of the men who wanted to form a trust to turnpike a very bad stretch of road in the Potteries, from Burslem to Church Lawton in Cheshire, which was on the good London road. Along this stretch raw materials and finished pottery had to be carried, but the road was so bad that in winter even pack horses could hardly travel on it. Goods coming to or from Liverpool to Burslem had to be sent south first to Newcastle-under-Lyme, which doubled the distance.

The innkeepers and shopkeepers of Newcastle naturally opposed the plan to improve the bad stretch, for they were afraid of losing valuable trade. However, by arguing that the interests of 150 different potteries and 7,000 workers were

The York Royal Mail Coach passing through a Toll Gate at night

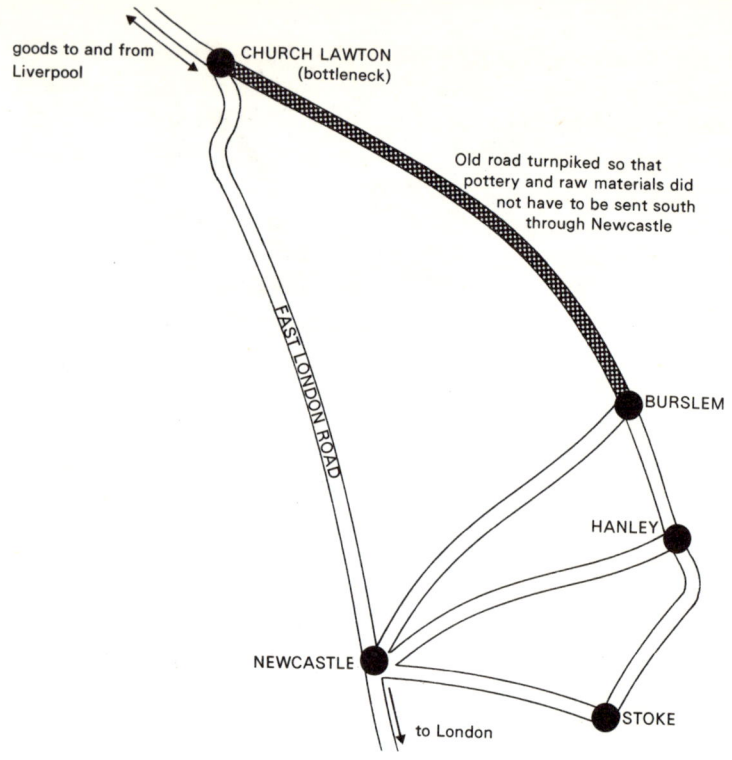

more important than those of a handful of tradesmen, Wedgwood succeeded, and in 1763 an Act of Parliament allowed a trust to be set up. The most serious 'bottle-neck' in the roads of the potteries could now be overcome.

CANALS

Despite these road improvements, heavy goods could still be carried much more cheaply on water than by land. Adam Smith, a famous writer on trade, stated that 'by sea, six or eight men can carry and bring back in the same time the same quantity of goods between London and Edinburgh, as fifty broad-wheeled wagons, attended by one hundred men, and drawn by four hundred horses'.

Not all important towns were near the coast or on navigable rivers, and Dutch and French engineers realised that artificial rivers, or canals, could be made to run exactly where they were needed. There were many problems to overcome, such as the need for locks to take canals up or down hills, the loss of water through leakage or evaporation, and the need for tunnels through high mountains.

In England canals were developed much later, and it was a nobleman who proved their practicality here. The Duke of Bridgewater had been very much impressed by the Languedoc canal in Southern France, which he had seen when on his Grand Tour. On his return to England he spent some time in London gambling, drinking and courting. But he was unlucky in love and at the age of twenty-three he decided to return to his estates in Lancashire.

On his lands at Worsley there was coal, and only seven miles away in Manchester there were many people eager to buy it. Yet the cost of taking the coal this seven miles increased the price so much that few could afford it. In 1759 Bridgewater decided to make a fortune and provide cheap coal at the same time by cutting a canal straight from the depths of his coalmines, which needed draining of water anyway, to Manchester.

He was helped by his estate agent, John Gilbert, and by a very clever *millwright*, James Brindley, who had already worked for Wedgwood at Etruria. There was much opposition to the idea of the canal, and many difficulties. Bridgewater had to promise not to charge more than 4*d* per hundredweight for his coal when the canal was opened, before Parliament would grant him permission to begin it. Brindley had to overcome many geographical problems – the most impressive engineering feat being the taking of the canal across the River Irwell. Bridgewater did not want to have to connect his canal to this river for this would have meant coming under the control of the company which charged for transport on it – and since they were against the canal anyway, they would have charged excessively high prices for the use of a short stretch of the river. Brindley solved the problem by taking the canal across the river by an aqueduct at Barton. This aqueduct very nearly cracked and crumbled when it was first filled with water, almost justifying

The Bridgewater Canal at Barton Bridge in 1814. This was the most spectacular engineering feat on the canal

the scoffers who laughed at the Duke and his engineer for 'building castles in the air'. It was quickly strengthened, however, and finally held.

The price of coal was halved in Manchester, and Bridgewater quickly planned to extend the canal to Liverpool. In the Midlands, an area handicapped by transport problems, businessmen began to take these new canals or 'inland navigations' much more seriously. Wedgwood became very interested in a plan to link the Trent and Mersey rivers by canal, which would connect the Potteries to Liverpool. He called in Brindley to ask his advice, and they began to discuss the best route for the canal.

Bridgewater realised that if he could persuade Wedgwood to link this proposed 'Grand Trunk' canal with his own canal, many more merchants would use both of them. On 6 July 1765 Wedgwood visited the Duke and was taken on a tour of his estates. Josiah wrote proudly:

> I have been waiting upon his Grace the Duke of Bridgewater with plans respecting the Inland Navigation – Mr Sparrow went along with me, and we were most graciously received and spent about eight hours in his Grace's company. . . .

A canal meeting. Note the heated argument about the plan of the proposed canal. The man on the right is reading a 'Report of the Engineer concerning the Andes Canal'

After his Grace had dismissed us we had the honour, and pleasure too, of sailing in his *Gondola* nine miles along his canal, through a most delightful vale to Manchester.

Josiah was also very pleased because the Duke had ordered 'the completest Table service of cream colour that I could make'. This set cost £160, which the Duke could hardly afford, for he was already deeply in debt due to the high costs of canal cutting. However, through the order he had gained a valuable and enthusiastic supporter, and fortunately his debts were easily paid out of the future profits made by his canal.

Wedgwood set to work to try to persuade the rich and important to support the new canal. On 20th December 1765 James Brindley noted that, 'Wadgwood of Burslem came to Dunham and sent for mee and we dined with Lord Grey and Sir Harry Mainwaring and others'. (Brindley was a bad speller but a brilliant engineer). Josiah was busy trying to argue for the canal – but he did not convince everyone, for Brindley also tells us that, 'Sir Harry could not keep his temper'.

Nine days later a general meeting was called to discuss the canal. Brindley outlined the plans for 93½ miles of waterway, 95 with seventy-three locks and a tunnel two miles long piercing the high ridge at Harecastle. Twenty-three miles of branch lines were to connect important towns to the main canal, and Josiah made certain that one of these branches would run straight through the Ridgeway estate which he was planning to buy for his new works.

The meeting voted to ask Parliament to allow them to construct the canal. Earl Gower, who was Chairman, noticed Josiah's enthusiasm for the idea and asked him rather sharply what he was prepared to do in practice to support the canal. Wedgwood immediately offered £1,000 towards first expenses and promised to buy many 'shares' in it. The money to pay for the canal was found by offering for sale parts of the estimated cost. These gave the buyer a right to part of any future profits made by the canal (the amount of the profit depended upon how much of the total cost the buyer had supplied). For the building of the Trent and Mersey canal, five hundred shares were quickly sold for £200 each.

People who made money out of the old transport methods naturally fought against the canal. The opposition of road transporters, river companies, ship-owners, landowners and towns which might be left stranded by the canal was angrily expressed in Parliament. Josiah had to spend three months in London, anxiously persuading politicans to support the canal. He succeeded, and on 14 May 1766 the Trent and Mersey Canal Act was passed.

There was great rejoicing in the Potteries. In July Wedgwood himself cut the first sod of the new canal. At night a sheep was roasted whole in Burslem, and muskets were fired to celebrate the victory – some rather too close to Wedgwood's house. For Brindley the engineer, however, the problems had only just begun. He had to organise and control between 400 and 600 men scattered over miles of country. Very difficult work was sometimes given to men who promised to build a certain lock or bridge for a sum of money fixed in advance. To dig the main stretches, Brindley came to agreements with different groups of workers, usually paying them 3d each for every cubic yard of earth or stone removed. This hard work was not very well paid – a navigator or 'navvy' probably earned only about five shillings per week, plus food and lodging.

Many very skilled craftsmen were also needed – brickmakers and bricklayers, quarrymen, miners and tunnellers. Special barges were fitted out with elaborate equipment, so that these craftsmen could continue work as the canal moved slowly forward. Brindley was very good at overcoming any special snags or difficulties, and he made clever use of all available building material. A letter from an inhabitant of Burslem in 1767 shows this clearly: 'Brindley has cut a mile through bogs, which he binds up, embanking them with stones which he gets out of other parts of the navigation. The clay he cuts out serves for bricks.'

The canal took eleven years to complete, but Brindley died before the most difficult section, Harecastle tunnel, was finished. However, Wedgwood's confidence and enthusiasm were well rewarded. In 1792 the cost of sending goods from Etruria to Liverpool had been cut from 10d to 1$\frac{1}{2}d$ per ton for every mile, and those who had bought shares in the canal received very good profits.

SHIPS

From Liverpool, Hull, London, or Bristol Wedgwood's pottery was taken in ships to the four corners of the world. In this section you can read about the ships in which Josiah sent out so much of his pottery.

Timber was still the main material used in ship-building in the eighteenth century. Fittings such as anchors were made out of iron, but iron ships did not become common until well into the nineteenth century. The other great change, which was the use of steam power, was also not applied extensively until after 1800. Wood and sail remained popular until well after 1850. Indeed the great fear of the late eighteenth century was that timber supplies might run out. In 1804 Admiral Collingwood advised all farmers 'to walk through their farms with a pocketful of acorns to drop in the side-hedges'. Unfortunately this 97

Shipbuilding on the Howland Great Dock near Deptford

advice was rather like shutting the stable door after the horse has bolted, for an oak takes about a hundred years to grow.

In the eighteenth century the number of ships constantly increased – a sign that trade was also increasing. In 1702 it was estimated that there was one quarter of a million tons of shipping in England. By 1793 there were one and a half million tons. Altogether by 1790 there were over four thousand ships involved in foreign trade. This rapid growth is reflected in the figures for individual ports:

Thousands of tons of shipping in leading English ports

	1702	1788
London	140	315
Newcastle	11	106
Liverpool	9	76
Sunderland	4	54
Whitehaven	7	52
Hull	8	52
Whitby	8	50
Bristol	17	38
Yarmouth	10	36

The most important changes in the design of ships and the way they were built came from the attempt to cut down the numbers of men needed to sail them. The cost of sea transport, after the first expense of building the ship, was mainly in the wages and food of the crew. If the crew could be cut down, the charges to the merchants could be reduced, so that they would send more and more goods by sea. Flat, long ships – like oblong boxes – were therefore built, copying the designs of Norwegian and Dutch coasting ships and the Newcastle *colliers*. These merchant ships were very slow. It still took eight or nine weeks to cross the Atlantic in 1790, just as long as it had taken the Pilgrim Fathers when they sailed to America one hundred and seventy years earlier.

However, such slow ships were very safe, they could hold more and more cargo, and they could be sailed by fewer men. A ship of 130 tons in 1630 had needed a crew of eighteen or nine-

The Old East India Docks – notice the many different cargoes, the clerk checking off a cargo, and the coopers making barrels

teen men. By 1760 this crew need be only eight or nine. A 200 ton Virginian trader which once needed twenty men to sail her had a crew of only thirteen by 1760.

Trade was now increasing so much that ship-owners were no longer afraid to build very large ships. There was little danger of them standing idle waiting for cargo or sailing half-empty. Although most merchant ships were still less than 200 tons, merchants knew that it was cheaper to use large ships whenever possible, for by 1760 the wage and food costs of a large ship were not very much more than the costs of a ship only half the size.

What was life like on board these ships? It would obviously vary from ship to ship – conditions on a large 'East Indiaman', of over 1,000 tons, which sailed on a two year voyage with a crew of 100, were very different from those on a small collier sailing between London and Newcastle many times a year. Every ship, however, would have a master or captain, and a mate. They had to make sure that the ship was sailed to the right place. Methods of telling where a ship was when at sea were improving – instruments such as the *compass* and *chronometer* became more reliable – but very often the master relied on his own knowledge of the coasts to which he was sailing.

Masters often made mistakes. In 1731, for example, an unfortunate Captain Williams, returning from the West Indies, took his ship up the Bristol Channel instead of the English Channel. The owner of the ship was justifiably annoyed and complained: 'How in the world you could commit such a blunder I can't imagine, now in the summer when it's not bad weather and near seventeen hours daylight. Can't remember of any such mistake made by anyone in my life at that time of the year.'

Most ships carried other skilled men besides the master. A ship's carpenter was needed. A cook and a doctor were very important on a long voyage. The boatswain was the expert in matters of sail and rigging, and he was foreman over the rest of the crew, who were either ordinary seamen or unskilled 'landsmen', numbers depending on the size of the ship.

Life at sea could be dangerous. Pirates were still one risk. Wrecks and sinkings were common, because there were no lifeboats and very few lighthouses or buoys to warn sailors of rocky coasts. Disasters at sea sometimes happened when least expected – in 1782 the 'Royal George' sank in Portsmouth harbour with 800 men and 400 women on board, and there were few survivors. Seven years later the 'Adventure' was wrecked off Newcastle and the entire crew drowned in sight of land.

Horrible tales were told about the food on these ships. No doubt the bread sometimes was full of maggots, the cheese so hard that buttons could be made out of it, the meat rotten and the beer stale. No doubt a sailor's food appears very uninteresting and unappetising to us. Yet food in merchant ships was much better than that in the royal navy. A diet of salt beef or pork, biscuits, cheese, dried fish and beer was probably richer and more varied than that which most men ate on land.

There were also stories about cruelty and brutality on board ships. The sad tale of a mistake made by a chief mate named John Cramer does show that violence must have been very much an everyday matter. He admitted before a Law Court that, 'One evening being dark, and calling all hands on deck 101 in a hurry, the captain being the last, I by mistake struck him, taking him to be a common fellow; insomuch as I gave him two black eyes and he never forgave me afterward.'

If conditions on board both merchant and fighting ships were bad, how did the merchant shipowners manage to find men willing to become sailors? In the first place, the wages were high. Often an unskilled seaman could earn more than a skilled craftsman on land. They received their wages in a lump sum at the end of a voyage and the amount would vary according to the profits made on the voyage. Although many sailors would squander their money on drink, others must have saved up enough to set themselves up in a small business when they decided that they had had enough of wandering.

Travel and adventure must have been a second attraction of life at sea. A sailor had the chance to see flying fish in the tropics, bask in the sun in the Mediterranean, visit the mysterious East and the exciting West. He might also have to face fogs and gales in the Baltic, but this would usually be either ignored or forgotten by young men who were eager to see the world.

The final pull of the sea was in the likely chance of rapid promotion. A serious and hard-working young man had an excellent chance of bettering himself on a merchant ship. If he was very lucky or very skilful he might even become master of his own ship. This would give him far more power and money than he could hope to obtain if he stayed at home.

A sailor's life had many hardships, but for an ambitious youth these were more than balanced by its attractions. You might like to discuss which life you would have liked best – the sailor's or the pottery worker's at Etruria?

WEDGWOOD'S POLITICAL IDEAS

Although improvements in transport were welcomed by both the old nobility and the newly rich manufacturers such as Wedgwood, there were other subjects on which they argued violently. Josiah disagreed with his noble customers on many important questions. For example, he believed that the system of representation in Parliament was very unfair, since it gave

too much importance to the rich and noble. Wedgwood stated quite firmly in 1780, 'every member of the state must either have a vote or be a slave.'

Josiah was an active member of the 'Society for *Suppression* of the Slave Trade', formed in 1787 to end this cruel practice. Wedgwood gave the movement much publicity when he made the famous *cameo* of the kneeling slave, who asked 'Am I not a man and a brother?' These were distributed free of charge.

Wedgwood made a great deal of money out of trade with North America, and when the American colonists decided to break away from Britain, he supported their revolt quite firmly. When we tried to stamp out the revolt by force Wedgwood realised that this was impossible, and told Thomas Bentley on 8 January 1775: 'All the world are with the *minister* and against the poor Americans – They have all gone mad and I have given them up for incurables.' He compared our relations with America to those of a parent and child, but observed that the colonists had good reasons to revolt – 'we had driven out the brat in his infancy, and exposed him to wild beasts and savages, until we imagined he might be able to provide us some service.' 103

We then took him again under our parental protection; provided him with a *straight waistcoat*, and whenever he wriggled, drew it up a hole tighter.' Josiah argued that there was little wonder the Americans wished to be free from our control, and his views were justified by later events. For after the Americans had won their freedom, our trade with them actually increased.

Wedgwood also greeted the French revolution with great joy, 'rejoicing at the glorious blow struck for freedom'. When events in France became violent, however, his enthusiasm died away – like that of many other middle-class men.

Josiah Wedgwood was therefore a man of very wide interests in both industry and politics. He led the fight to improve roads and develop canals in the Potteries. He was the main influence behind the General Chamber of Manufacturers of Great Britain in 1785 to 1787. He had advanced views on many political topics. A final example of his determination to bring about improvements is his unsuccessful attempt to begin in 1775 a kind of *research* organisation into the practical chemical problems facing the potters of Staffordshire. This early idea of a joint scientific inquiry into industrial problems failed because Josiah could not persuade the other potters that such study was important enough for them to spend money on it. As usual, however, Wedgwood's ideas led him to find further ways of making money for himself. His interest in chemistry made him realise the need for improved laboratory apparatus, so that he soon developed a fast selling supply of pot mortars and pestles (for mixing materials), crucibles, tubes and dishes.

Wedgwood was never completely free from pain. He had trouble with his eyes, his chest and his leg, and he died on 3 January 1795 after a short illness. After this the business was carried on by his nephew, Thomas Byerley, and his son Josiah. They had troubles, especially during the wars with France which lasted until 1815, but they kept the firm going successfully.

11   Secrets of Success

'Wedgwood and Company' still make pottery today, although the firm is no longer completely owned by the Wedgwood family. In 1940 a new factory was built at Barlaston, and 2,500 men and women now work there. Of course there have been many changes. The ovens are now fired electrically and machines are used much more – such as the automatic cup-maker which shapes a cup every six seconds. However, the most famous Wedgwood pottery is still 'Jasperware', and its white decorations or reliefs are made and applied in much the same way today as they were nearly two hundred years ago.

Why was Josiah Wedgwood so successful? He was an expert potter who understood the practical problems of the industry, and he was always trying to improve quality by experimenting with different clays. His hard work was rewarded by two important new wares – Queen's Ware, the useful cream colour pottery, and Jasper ware, which was both useful and ornamental.

His partner, Thomas Bentley, helped him to sell his pottery to the rich, the famous and the fashionable. This success amongst the nobility ensured that, in an age of growing population and changing tastes, his pottery would also be eagerly bought by the middle classes.

Wedgwood was a great organiser. He cut his transport costs and improved his methods of selling. He made his workers more reliable and skilful by dividing up the processes of pottery manufacture and increasing their specialisation. He paid attention to the smallest detail and would always try to solve the slightest problem. He insisted on high quality. The most famous story told about Josiah Wedgwood is probably still a good explanation of his success. Wedgwood would walk round Etruria after his workers had gone home, inspecting the pottery and smashing any badly made ware with his stick. He then chalked on the bench, 'That won't do for Josiah Wedgwood'. Josiah set himself high standards and he expected his workers to do the same.

He also expected and received high profits. By 1795 his pottery was used all over the world. His customers included Spanish ambassadors, Italian Kings, German professors, Bohemian nobles, American merchants, and Englishmen in Canada and India.

His influence in the potteries was immense. When John Wesley had tried to preach in Burslem in 1760 he was stoned by an angry and savage mob. Twenty years later he wrote:

'I returned to Burslem. How is the whole face of the country changed in twenty years! The wilderness is a fruitful field. Houses, villages, towns have sprung up, and the people are improved as much as the country'.

He could have added that much of the improvement was due to the life and work of one man – Josiah Wedgwood.

How Do We Know?

Before the telephone, radio, television and cheap newspapers were available to spread news quickly, letter writing was a much more popular way of telling other people what was happening. Josiah Wedgwood wrote many letters, and the ones which tell us most about his business are those to Thomas Bentley. Unfortunately nearly all Bentley's replies have been lost, despite the fact that Josiah valued them so much that he had them bound together so that he could read them again.

At the modern Wedgwood factory at Barlaston many old documents and records from the earliest days of the firm are kept. Some of these, and examples of the early pottery, are displayed in a long gallery there.

The letters and diaries of many other famous eighteenth century figures are published in easily available books. In two or three years you may enjoy reading these – look for the names of Daniel Defoe, Parson Woodforde, Horace Walpole, Lord Hervey, Arthur Young and John Wesley.

Things to Do

FURTHER READING

There are many other interesting 'Then and There' books on this period, such as 'London in the Eighteenth Century', 'Bath in the Eighteenth Century', 'Roads and Canals In the Eighteenth Century', 'The Agrarian Revolution', 'A Border Woollen Town In The Industrial Revolution', 'A Textile Community in the Industrial Revolution', 'A Coal and Iron Community In the Industrial Revolution', and 'The Railway Revolution'. Most libraries contain general books and guides on pottery, and you will find the books of W. B. Honey useful.

1. Make a diagram or wall chart explaining and describing the different stages in pottery making. If you have the chance, try to make a simple piece of pottery yourself.

2. If there is a local pottery near your home, visit it. A visit to the modern Wedgwood factory at Barlaston is very interesting.

3. Find out about the work of other Staffordshire potters such as Enoch Booth, Ralph Wood, and Josiah Spode.

4. Find out as much as you can about ancient Greek pottery. Do you think Wedgwood was right in admiring it so much?

5. How does modern advertising on television and in the press try to appeal to 'snobbery'? Find actual examples.

6. Try to visit one of the famous eighteenth-century noble houses – Castle Howard, Woburn Abbey, Blenheim Palace are good examples, but there are many more.

7. Josiah Wedgwood built his home, Etruria Hall, very close to his pottery works. Would a modern factory owner do the same?

8. Write a conversation between an innkeeper in Newcastle and a potter in Burslem discussing the advantages and disadvantages of turnpike roads.

9. Find out how a lock works. Has your area any canals? Find out if they are still used by industries.

10. How does the life of a modern apprentice differ from that of an apprentice in 1760?
11. Which school rules do you agree or disagree with? Which factory rules would you have agreed or disagreed with?
12. Write a letter describing your imaginary experiences in the food riots of 1783.
13. Visit a big china shop and see if you can recognise the Wedgwood china.

Transcript for contract p. 49.

On these conditions I promise to build and complete two dwelling houses for Josiah Wedgwood agreeable to the particulars of the estimate no. 1 in this book in a good workmanlike manner for the sum of sixty-five pounds paid to me by the said J. Wedgwood when the houses are finished which is to be in four months from the date hereof on the penalty of forfeiting five pounds, that is to say if they are not finished in that time then the undertaker is to receive sixty pounds only for the two houses, and it is further agreed that if there is any brick used in the walls which fail or do not stand the weather that then the said under-taker shall replace such brick at his own expense. In witness of the above agreements we have hereunto set our hands, the 31st of May 1769 –

JOSIAH WEDGWOOD
THOS. SHAW

Glossary

This is a list of difficult words, some of which are not very much used today. If the word you want to know is not here, look it up in a dictionary.

accountant, an expert on business matters who checks records of sales

to admonish, to warn or threaten

apparel, clothing

apprentice, young person learning a trade, hence *apprenticed*, placed as an apprentice.

architect, designer of buildings

archaeologist, one who studies the distant past, by digging up its remains

authorised, told to do something, set an example by

bankrupts, people who have failed in business and cannot pay their debts

biscuit, pottery once-fired but unglazed

cameo, carving in one layer of coloured stone against a background of another colour

chronometer, extremely accurate clock

cobbled, paved with rounded stones

colliers, coal ships, miners

compass, instrument used to find north

consumption, buying and using

depopulation, fewer people living in a place

discipline, rules to bring better behaviour.

to disperse, scatter, go away.

écritoire, pen-and-ink stand

engages, promises

to err, to make a mistake

esteemed, valued

ewer, water-jug

fob pocket, small pocket to hold watch

forfeit, penalty, fine

fossilling, searching for fossils (the hardened remains of plants and animals which lived thousands of years ago)

glaze, shiny surface of twice-baked pottery or china

gondola, flat boat

millwright, a man who made water-wheels (the first engineers)

minister, politician in charge of a department

octagonal, eight-sided

option, choice

pewter, metal, mixture of tin, copper and lead

plaster of Paris, chalky, calcium substance which holds water

pyrometer, instrument for measuring very high temperatures

relief, decoration projecting (sticking out) from pottery or stone etc.

reputation, what other people think about somebody

research, detailed study of new problems

shoals, large numbers together (like whales)

slip, semifluid clay for coating or making patterns on earthenware

sod, a square of turf

subsidence, ground sinking

suppression, stopping, ending

sterling, of great value

storey, horizontal division or floor of a building (1st floor, 2nd floor etc.)

straight waistcoat, jacket used to confine someone's arms (either in very long sleeves tied together, or strapped inside the jacket).

to throw, to shape soft clay on a turning wheel

toll, charge made to travel on a road

tureens, large dishes, usually for soup

universally, everywhere

vies, competes with, imitates

wager, a bet or gamble

ware, general name given to pottery (e.g. earthenware, stoneware)

Acknowledgements

The author would like to thank Josiah Wedgwood and Sons Ltd. and Mr. W. Billington, Curator of the Wedgwood Museum at the factory, for their generous help, and the author and publisher are grateful to the following for permission to reproduce copyright material: Hutchinson Publishing Group Limited for three extracts from *Portraits and Documents*; *Eighteenth Century*; Josiah Wedgwood & Sons Limited for various extracts from Wedgwood letters.

For permission to reproduce illustrative material we are grateful to the following:

Page		Page	
frontis	Josiah Wedgwood and Sons Ltd. (Wedgwood)	25	Wedgwood
		28	Wedgwood
6	*both* British Museum (B.M.)	29	E. Meteyard *Life of Josiah Wedgwood vol II*, Hurst and Blackett, 1866
8	B.M.		
9	Victoria and Albert Museum	30	Wedgwood
		31	Blakes, Stoke-on-Trent
13	Wedgwood	34	R.T.H.P.L.
15	Radio Times Hulton Picture Library (R.T.H.P.L.)	35	Wedgwood
		36	*top* Wedgwood
			bottom R.T.H.P.L.
16	From Goodwood House by Courtesy of the Trustees	37	Wedgwood
		38	Wedgwood
18	*top* R.T.H.P.L.	39	*both* Wedgwood
	bottom Victoria and Albert Museum	40	Wedgwood
		48	Longman Group Ltd.
20	Wedgwood	49	Wedgwood Museum Trust, Barlaston
21	Wedgwood Museum Trust, Barlaston		
		50	Mansell Collection
22	Wedgwood	52	R.T.H.P.L.
23	Wedgwood	53	National Portrait Gallery